THE
NEW LATIN AMERICAN
CINEMA

THE
NEW LATIN AMERICAN
CINEMA

An annotated bibliography of sources in
English, Spanish, and Portuguese:
1960-1980

Compiled by
JULIANNE BURTON

SMYRNA PRESS
NEW YORK, N. Y.

Library of Congress No. 83-080377

ISBN 0-918266-17-3

This bibliography was produced in cooperation with *Cineaste* magazine. Particular thanks to Gary Crowdus, Lenny Rubenstein, Elyse Dayton, and Dan Georgakas.

SMYRNA PRESS
Box 1803-GPO
Brooklyn, NY 11202

TABLE OF CONTENTS

FOREWORD

This bibliography is designed as a research guide to historical, theoretical, and critical works on Latin American cinema. It expands and updates an earlier edition published by *Cineaste* in 1976. In my foreword to the first edition, I explained that my undertaking grew out of the increased availability of Latin American films and a growing interest in the United States and Canada in politically-committed Latin American filmmaking. I expressed the hope that "this guide will stimulate more extensive use of the available films, eventually encouraging the importation of additional films and generating more film criicism and scholarship."

The response from film students, programmers, educators, and community organizers to the first edition has been enthusiastic. The number of Latin American films available in North America continue to grow and the number of English language articles on Latin American film has more than doubled. An even more disproportionate growth of film-related publishing in Spanish and Portuguese is evidenced in the greatly expanded list of book-length studies that follows.

Although the intervening years have been difficult ones for political filmmakers in most Latin American countries, Brazil and Cuba continue to produce films of great interest and appeal while exiled Chilean filmmakers, despite their dispersal, have begun to explore more generalized issues without abandoning concern for their nation's fate. In countries like Venezuela and Nicaragua, filmmaking is on the rise and filmmakers in other countries (Colombia, Argentina, Peru) continue to struggle against sobering but not yet impossible odds. This same period has also seen a marked increase in filmmaking in Spanish speaking communities within the United States large enough to warrant the inclusion of a section on Chicano, Puerto Rican, and exiled Cuban filmmaking in this edition.

Descriptions of approximately 150 articles constitute the bulk of this edition. The initial general listing is divided chronologically and within each year, alphabetically by the author's last name. Subsequent sections cover film production in nine Latin American countries (listed alphabetically) and the Hispanic cinema in the U.S. Again, articles are organized according to year of publication and within any given year, alphabetically according to the author's last name. Particularly prolific national film industries are further divided into sections on individual directors. These subsections are first organized alphabetically by director, then chronologically, and finally alphabetically by author. Relevant sections of books dedicated to broader topics are treated as articles and listed accordingly. An effort has been made to distinguish reviews from genuine film history and criticism and to exclude the former in favor of the latter, although exceptions have been made for reviews of exceptional scope or importance.

In order to encourage those who wish to go beyond the growing number of sources in English, I have included summaries of major books in Spanish and Portuguese and descriptions of the most relevant film magazines currently published in Latin America. As an aid to ongoing research, I have also listed English-language journals which cover Latin American film activity with some regularity. To make the bibliography as practical as possible, I have included reference guides to current addresses of distributors and periodicals.

I am grateful to Don Wohlfeiler and Patricia McClanahan, former students of mine at the University of California at Santa Cruz(for their assistance during the initial stages of this revised bibliography. In addition, I extend special thanks to Jesus Trevino for generously supplying me with material on Chicano cinema. I am also indebted to the Social Science Research Council for a grant that enabled me to finish this undertaking while simultaneously initiating other more sustained and original work. A final thanks to the *Cineaste* staff for its assistance in making possible the original and now revised edition of this bibliography.

JULIANNE BURTON

BIBLIOGRAPHIES

MITRY JEAN, compiler. *Bibliographie internationale du cinéma et de la television*, vol. 3. *Espagne. Portugal et pays de langue espagnole ou portugaise.* Paris: Institut des Hautes Études Cinématographiques (IDHEC). 1968. 163 pp.

An annotated bibliography of book-length sources in Spanish and Portuguese, organized in six sections: bibliography, history of the cinema, aesthetics, technique, festivals and biography.

E. BRADFORD BURNS, "Film," *Handbook of Latin American Studies* No. 38, Gainesville: University of Florida Press in conjunction with The Library of Congress, 1976, pp. 59-69.

First general bibliography on Latin American film to be included in this key sourcebook for Latin American Studies. Includes works in Spanish and Portuguese as well as English.

JULIANNE BURTON, "Film: Revolutionary Cuban Cinema," *Handbook of Latin American Studies* No. 39, Gainesville: University of Florida Press in conjunction with The Library of Congress, 1977, pp. 425-434.

This annotated bibliography includes works in Spanish, Italian and German as well as English.

JULIANNE BURTON, "Film," *Handbook of Latin American Studies* No. 40, Gainesville: University of Florida Press in conjunction with The Library of Congress, 1978, pp. 57-67.

Annotated. Covers works in Spanish, Portuguese and other European languages, as well as English.

FILMOGRAPHIES

GENERAL

JANE M. LOY, *Latin America: Sights and Sounds, A Guide to Motion Pictures and Music for College Courses* (CLASP Pamphlet No. 5, Latin American Studies Association, Box 13362, University Station, Gainesville, FL 32604). 1973. 243 pp.

A useful guide to films from the U.S. as well as Latin America with descriptions of each and suggested complementary readings. Thoughtfully prepared and carefully indexed.

(no author given) "Filmografia," *Octubre* (Mexico), No. 2, January 1975 pp. 52-55.

Lists directors and countries of origin for the most important films of the new Latin American cinema movement from 1955 through 1974.

HELEN W. CYR, *A Filmography of the Third World: An Annotated List of 16mm Films* (Metuchen, New Jersey: Scarecrow Press). 1976. 319 pp.

Listings—by region and country—are far from complete, but useful nonetheless. Includes a directory of distributors.

SUSAN J. HIGGINS, compiler, *A Latin American Filmography*, The University of Texas at Austin: Institute of Latin American Studies, 1978, 132 pp.

Designed as an access guide for junior and community colleges, this filmography provides descriptions of films from and about Latin America (organized both by topic and by country). In addition, listings of filmstrips, videotapes and slide presentations are included, along with annotated bibliographical information and directories of distributors.

ARLENE MOSCOVITCH, compiler, *Latin America: A Filmography*, Toronto, Ontario: National Film Board of Canada, n.d. (Nov., 1979).

A listing of audio-visual materials from and about Latin America available in metropolitan Toronto.

PATRICIA PEYTON, ed., *Reel Change*, The Film Fund, 1979, 141 pp., illus.

An annotated filmography of social issue films, organized by topic, with a proportion of listings from Latin America and about Latino communities in the U.S.

TERESA TOLEDO, compiler, *Filmes Latinoamericanos: Una cronologia tentativa, 1960-1979,* Cinemateca de Cuba, Seccion de Cine Latinoamericano y del Caribe: Havana, November, 1980. 45 pp.
Organized into two parts, fictional and documentary cinema, this filmography is then further divided alphabetically into countries and chronologically within each country's film production. Information is limited to date, title and author. The compiler's introduction stresses that this is a working filmography, preliminary to a more definitive *Catalogo del Nuevo Cine Latinoamericano.*

BRAZIL

RANDAL JOHNSON AND ROBERT STAM, "Brazilian Renaissance: Annotated Filmography," *Jump/Cut* Special Section "Brazilian Renaissance," Part II, *Jump/Cut: A Review of Contemporary Cinema* No. 22, May, 1980, pp. 22-24, illus.

Brief reviews of thirteen post-Cinema Novo feature films (made between 1972 and 1978) with a guide to U.S. distributors.

CHICANO

CYNTHIA BAIRD, *La Raza in Films: A List of Films and Filmstrips,* California: Oakland Public Library. (Supplement: 1974.)

Annotated list of films and filmstrips covering Mexico, Latin America, and Spanish-speaking populations in the U.S.

RUBEN GARCIA, compiler, *La Raza Film Bibliography,* Santa Barbara: La Causa Publications, 1976.

Listing of films accompanied by introductory essays on La Raza history.

CUBA

MARIA EULALIA DOUGLAS, compiler, *Filmografia del cine cubano,*

1959-junio, 1980, Havana Cinemateca de Cuba: Seccion de Cine Cubano, October, 1980, 88 pp.

Organized chronologically, with each year subdivided into Documentary Films, Fictional Films, and Animated Films. In addition to date, title and director, this filmography also provides the duration of each film and a brief description.

BOOKS—SPANISH AND PORTUGUESE

GENERAL

AUGUSTO MARTINEZ AND MANUEL PEREZ ESTREMERA, *Nuevo cine Latinoamericano* (Calle de la Cruz, 44, Barcelona 17: Editorial Anagrama, 1973). 226 pp.

This book traces the development of cinema from its inception through 1972 in nine Latin American countries (Argentina, Bolivia, Brazil, Chile, Colombia, Cuba, Mexico, Peru and Venezuela) and includes some brief notes on the situation in some less cinematographically developed nations. The approach is a compromise between cinematographic historiography and critical appraisal, since the authors take care to situate films, filmmakers and film movements in their specific historical and social context before offering critical evaluations of the films themselves. Schematic filmographies at the end of each chapter provide a useful aid, but the book shortchanges the serious scholar by omitting index and bibliography. Unfortunately, factual errors abound.

GALINDO, ALEJANDRO, *¿Qué es el cine?* (Mexico: Editorial. Nuestro Tiempo). 1975. 149 pp.

A leading Mexican director discusses filmmaking in general and Mexico's in particular in a series of essays.

GUY HENNEBELLE, ed., *Quinze ans de cinema mondial: 1960-1975* (Paris: editions du Cerf). 1975. 425 pp.

_____ *Los cines nacionales contra Hollywood* (Valencia: Fernando Torres), 1977, vol. I: 261 pp.; vol. II: 263-559, illus.

A polemical collection of essays concerning the development of alternative cinema, especially in the Third World. The section on Latin America contains brief accounts of filmmaking activity in Argentina, Bolivia, Colombia, Peru, Uruguay, Mexico and Chile, and slightly longer essays on Cuba and Brazil.

RENE PALACIOS MORE AND DANIEL MATEUS, *El cine Latinoamericano O por una estetica de la ferocidad, la magia y la violencia* (Madrid: Sedmany Editores). 1976. 192 pp., illus.

The first third of this volume consists of a "dialogue" between its two authors, both Argentine filmmakers, on topics ranging from cultural dependency and commercial cinema to "liberation cinema." The remaining portion contains a fine selection of theoretical writings by a dozen prominent Latin American filmmakers.

(Coleccion Cine Rocinante No. 5)—*Por un cine Latinoamericano*, Vol. II, Caracas: Rocinante, 1978, 142 pp., illus.

A compilation of reports and declarations from the Fifth Meeting of the Committee on Latin American Filmmakers, held in Merida, Venezuela in April of 1977.

ARMAND MATTELART AND HECTOR SCHMUCLER, editors, "El cine en America Latina" (special issue), *Comunicacion y cultura*, vol. 5, March 1978 (Mexico, D.F.: Editorial Nueva Imagen), 194 pp.

Includes an interview with Emilio Garica Riera on New Cinema in Mexico, and articles on "Transnational Influence in Argentine Cinema," Argentine ethnographic filmmaker Jorge Preloran, Eisenstein in Mexico, the fifth meeting of the Latin American Filmmakers' Committee, and Octavio Getino on "The Film Industry in Latin America."

ALFONSO GUMUCIO DAGRON, editor, *Cine, Censura y Exilio en America Latina*, La Paz, Bolivia: Ediciones Film/historia, 1979, 153 pp., illus.

The question on censorship and repression in the Latin American film sector is addressed through articles and interviews by the editor and others. Seven countries are represented with separate chapters (Argentina, Bolivia, Brazil, Chile, Colombia, Mexico, and Peru) while countries like Uruguay, Venezuela, Haiti and Cuba are left for a final section on "Other Countries."

ISAAC LEON FRIAS, compiler, *Los años de la conmocion, 1967-1973: Entrevistas con realizadores sudamericanos* (Mexico: Direccion General de Difusion Cultural de la UNAM) [Cuadernos de Cine No. 28]. 1979. 293 pp., illus.

A collection of interviews from the Peruvian film journal *Hablemos de cine*, beginning with a roundtable discussion between Gustavo Dahl (Brazil), Tomas Gutierrez Alea (Cuba), and Fernando Solanas (Argentina). Filmmakers represented are: E. Cozarinsky, L. Torre Nilsson, J. Sanjines, C. Diegues, R. Guerra, L. Hirszman, N. Pereira dos Santos, G. Rocha, C. Alvarez, M. Littin, R. Ruiz, and M. Handler.

JULIAN DEL MONTE Y FERNANDO CAMPOS, editors, *Anuario Ibero-americano de cine y television, 1979* (Madrid: Equipo Cordillera). 1980. 528 pp., illus.

The first of what promises to be an eminently useful annual publication on the order of the *International Film Guide*, but limited in this case to the Spanish-speaking world. Part I contains technical information and a brief description of feature film and television production in fifteen Luso-hispanic countries. Part II contains a directory of film and television producers, studios and laboratories, organized alphabetically by country. Part III offers information on festivals, film archives, television channels, and brief summaries of the current situation for film production in all the countries featured.

FEE VAILLANT, editor, *Der Film Lateinamerikas: Eine Dokumentation/ El Cine en America Latina: Documentacion* (Retrospective, 29th International Film Week, Mannheim, Germany). Federal Ministry of Economic Collaboration: Bonn, 1980. 613 pp. (pp. 313-613 in Spanish or Portuguese), illus.

Essays by filmmakers and brief reviews of selected films. Countries represented include: Argentina, Bolivia, Brazil, Chile, Costa Rica, Colombia, Cuba, Mexico, Nicaragua, Panama, Peru, Uruguay and Venezuela.

ARGENTINA

FERNANDO E. SOLANAS AND OCTAVIO GETINO, *Cine, cultura y Decolonizacion* (Buenos Aires: Siglo XXI, 1973). 204 pp.

The selections in this anthology trace the activities and theoretical-artistic development of the Argentine *Cine Liberacion* group from its early work beginning in 1966 through its acclaimed film-essay *The Hour of the Furnaces* and up to 1972. Essays like "Hacia un tercer cine" ("Towards a Third Cinema") and "Apuntes para un juicio critico descolonizadi" ("Notes for a Decolonized Critical Criterion") have earned these filmmakers a place of theoretical prominence among committed filmmakers in Latin America.

JOSÉ Agustin MAHIEU, *Breve historia del cine argentino.* Buenos Aires: EUDEBA, 1966. 78 pp., fascim., illus.

A brief history of Argentine cinema from 1896 through the short-lived Argentine "New Wave" of the mid-1960s, including a chronology of key events (not to be confused with Agustin Mahieu's *Breve historia del cine nacional, 1896-1974*).

ALBERTO GIUDICI, *El cine argentino; Hollywood: del esplendor al ocaso,* Buenos Aires: Ediciones Accion, 1976? 80 pp., illus.

The first section in this double book provides a 25-p. "summary chronology" of Argentine cinema from its origins through the release of *La Patagonia rebelde* in 1973 to the almost total paralysis of the industry in 1975.

ULISES PETIT DE MURAT AND HOMERO MANZI, *Pampa barbara.* Buenos Aires: Conjunta Editores, 1976, 230 pp.

The screenplay of this now-classic 1945 feature on gaucho life directed by Lucas Demare and Hugo Fregonese. With an introduction ("Cuando Rosas y Lavalle eran amigos") by Homero Manzi.

JORGE ABEL, C. MARTIN, *Cine argentino '76.* Buenos Aires: Ediciones Metrocop. 1977. 87 pp.

A chronological summary of Argentine film production and legislation during 1976, followed by production credits for each film and directors' filmographies.

HOMERO ALSINA THEVENET, general editor, *Reportaje al cine argentino: Los pioneros del sonoro.* Buenos Aires: America Norildis Editores, 1978.

Interviews with filmmakers and actors, followed by a list of national films released in Argentina between 1933 and 1940.

OCTAVIO GETINO, *Cine y dependencia: El Cine en la Argentina.* Buenos Aires/Lima: "Cine Liberacion," 1976/1978, 124 pp. + (mimeograph, bound).

Chapters on the history of dependency in the Argentine film industry from 1886, infrastructures of dependency (production and distribution), the ideological aspects of dependency, integration into a broader continental "project," and film as a vehicle for popular memory. Appendices contain biofilmographies of the silent and sound periods, tables and statistics.

BOLIVIA

CARLOS D. MESA G., *El cine en Bolivia* (La Paz: Editorial Don Bosco de la Laz) 1976 (unnumbered pages) illus. (Cinemateca de la Paz: Inauguracion, I.)

Contains a brief history of Bolivian filmmaking, with primary emphasis on the *Grupo Ukamau*, followed by a schematic chronology and filmography.

CARLOS D. MESA G., BEATRIZ PALACIOS, JORRE SANJINES, ARTURO VON VACANO, et. al., *Cine boliviano: Del realizador al critico.* La Paz, Bolivia: Editorial Gisbert, 1979, 297 pp., illus.

An assortment of materials on Bolivian film including an introductory orientation by the lead editor, a roundtable discussion, interviews with

16

Jorge Sanjines and Antonio Equino, appraisals of *Chuquiago* (Equino) and *Fuera de aqui* (Sanjines) as well as three lesser known Bolivian films, a biofilmography of Bolivian directors and a list of feature-length films made in Bolivia between 1923 and 1978.

JORGE SANJINES Y EL GRUPO UKAMAU, *Teoria y Practica de un Cine Junto al Pueblo*. Mexico: Siglo XXI Editores, 1979, 250 pp., illus.

An overview of the formal and theoretical evolution of the Ukamau Group in their search for a revolutionary and popular cinema. Contains nearly one hundred pages of sketches, treatments, and screenplays for their best known films.

BRAZIL

GLAUBER ROCHA, *Revisao Critica do Cinema Brasileiro* (Editora Civilizacao Brasileira, Rua Sete de Setembro, 97, Rio de Janeiro, 1963). 147 pp.

Rocha, who started out as a film critic and historian, summarizes the history of Brazilian cinema from pioneer Humberto Mauro to the first stirrings of what would be called the Cinema Novo.

GLAUBER ROCHA, *Deus e o Diabo na Terra do So!* (Editora Civilizacao Brasileira, Rut Sete de Setembro, 97, Rio de Janeiro, 1965.)

Includes the screenplay of *Black God, White Devil* and essays on the film by Rocha and others.

GLAUBER ROCHA AND AUGUSTO MARTINEZ TORRES, *Glauber Rocha y "Cabezas Cortadas"* (Calle de la Cruz 44, Barcelona 17: Editorial Anagrama, 1970). 106 pp.

The screenplay for *Cabezas Cortadas* is accompanied by Torres' introduction and diary of the filming, as well as a selection of reprints of Rocha's declarations about Cinema Novo in general and his own films in particular.

PAULO EMILIO SALLES GOMES, *Humberto Mauro, Cataguases, Cinearte*. Sao Paulo: Editora Perspectiva [and] University de Sao Paulo. 1974. 475 pp.

A detailed critical biography of one of the principal pioneers of Brazilian cinema. Traces the influences of the social environment on the young filmmaker, analyzes his most important films in depth, and discusses the role of the magazine *Cinearte* in the development of Brazilian film.

17

MARIA RITA ELIEZER GALVAO, *Crônica do cinema paulistano*. Sao Paulo. Atica. 1975. 333 pp.

Traces the development of cinema in Sao Paulo from its inception through 1930, arguing that this regional cinema was initially a proletarian form of expression, having grown out of the working class theater of Italian immigrants. A major portion of the book consists of interviews with 15 major figures from the period.

FRANCISCO ALVES DOS SANTOS, *Cinema brasileiro 1975: entrevistas com cineastas brasileiros*. Curitiba, Brazil: Edicoes Paiol. 1975. 72 pp., ill.

Short interviews with seven young Brazilian filmmakers: Andre Luiz Oliveira, Guido Araujo, Joao Batista de Andrade, Olney Sao Paulo, Osvaldo Caldeira, Ozualdo Candeias, and Silvio Back.

ALBERTO SILVA, *Cinema e humanismo*. Rio: Pallas. 1975. 128 pp.

A rather superficial collection of articles on Brazilian and foreign cinema, from the *chanchada* to Glauber Rocha to Ingmar Bergman. Informed by a vague leftist ideology which rejects the "decadence" of much modern European cinema in favor of films which deal with "the people" and "the great human questions."

JOSE IGNACIO DE MELO SOUZA, *Retrospectiva do cinema brasileiro, 1975*. Sao Paulo: Kronos Grafica e Editora. 1975? 94 pp.

A catalogue of the Brazilian films screened in Sao Paulo between January and December 1975, with notes on market conditions, censorship, etc., and a bibliography of related publications.

VICENTE DE PAULA ARAUJO, *A bela epoca do cinema brasileiro*, Sao Paulo: Perspectiva. 1976. 414 pp.

A non-analytical chronicle of the development and dissemination of mass entertainment in Rio from the late 1800s through 1912, when foreign filmmaking began to dominate the national market. Important for its historical documentation.

JEAN-CLAUDE BERNARDET, *Brasil en tempo de cinema: ensaio sobre o cinema brasileiro de 1958 a 1966*. 2nd ed. Rio: Paz e Terra. 1977. 190 pp., illus.

Important re-edition of a seminal work on modern Brazilian cinema, originally published in 1967, which analyzes Cinema Novo as essentially a middle-class movement dealing with middle-class problems.

RUBENS EWALD FILHO, *Dicionario de cineastas*. Revisão por João Evangelista Franco and Dina de Deus. Sao Paulo: Global Editora e Distribuidora. 1977. 469 pp., illus.

Modeled after the book by French film historian Georges Sadoul, *Dictionnaire des cinéastes*, this useful guide lists the works of the major national and foreign filmmakers and producers whose work has been screened in Sao Paulo from the silent era through 1976. An appendix lists annual prizes awarded at the world's leading film competitions.

RAQUEL GERBER, ed., *Glauber Rocha*. Rio: Paz e Terra. 1977. 169 pp., illus.

Anthology of studies on the leading Cinema Novo director, ranging from an excellent overview of Rocha's role in the movement (Gerber) to a structuralist study of his films (Rene Gardies) to detailed analyses of two sequences from *Land in anguish*. (Three of the four studies are translated from the French.)

MOZART BAPTISTA BEMQUERER, editor, *Cultura* Special Film Issue. Brasilia: Ministerio da Educacao e Cultura. 1977. 127 pp., illus.

A handsomely designed volume which includes essays on historical topics, aesthetics, film music, documentary, film and literature, the film market, Brazilian film festivals, etc., some of them by figures associated with Cinema Novo (Maurice Capovilla, Alex Viany, David E. Neves, Gustavo Dahl).

MIRIAM ALENCAR, *O Cinema em festivais e os caminhos do curta-metragem no Brasil*. Rio de Janeiro: Editora Artenova & Embrafilme. 1978. 142 pp., illus.

A guide to national festivals and short film activity in Brazil.

JEAN-CLAUDE BERNARDET, *Cinema Brasileiro: Propostas para uma Historia*. Rio: Paz e Terra. 1979. 203 pp.

Brazil's leading critic addresses some of the key issues which have faced Brazilian cinema.

ALCINO TEIXEIRA DE MELLO, *Legislacao do Cinema Brasileiro*, Vol. 1: Legislacao Basica; Legislacao Complementar, Resolucoes do CONCINE; Vol. II: Resolucoes do INC, Convenios, Acordos, Planos, Instrucoes, Circulares, Portarias, Apendice. Rio de Janeiro: Embrafilme. 1978.

Compendia of legislation relating to all aspects of film in Brazil, by the president of CONCINE (National Film Council).

ZELITO VIANA, *Terra dos Indios*. Rio de Janeiro: Embrafilme e Mapa. 1979. 117 pp., illus.

A sequence-by-sequence reconstruction of this feature-length documentary, generously illustrated, including the director's recollections of the shooting.

19

CHILE

MARIO GODOY QUESADA, *Historia del cine chileno*. Santiago: 1966. A virtually year-by-year account of Chilean film production from 1902 through 1966.

FRANCESCO BOLZONI, *El cine de Allende* (Cirilo Amoros 71,Valencia 4, Spain: Fernando Torres editor, 1974). Originally published as *Il Cinema di Allende*, Marsilio Editori, Italy, 1974. 163 pp.

An overview of filmmaking under Allende which reproduces sections *de cine*, and the *Quadermos* from the Pesaro Mostra del Nuovo Cinema from the Chilean film magazine *Primer Plano*, the Peruvian *Hablemos* (1970 and 1972). Reprinted interviews with Miguel Littin, Raul Ruiz, Aldo Francia and Helvio Soto are supplemented by first-hand exchanges with the author.

MIGUEL LITTIN, *Cine chileno: La tierra prometida* (Apartado 14.363, Candelaria. Caracas: Rocimante). 1974. 70 pp.

Biographical notes on Miguel Littin are followed by the stream-of-consciousness narrative which served as the basis for the screenplay of *The Promised Land* "The First Manifesto of the Popular Unity Filmmakers" is reprinted, as are two interviews with Littin which originally appeared in *Cine cubano*, and Littin's "Popular Culture and Anti-Imperialist Struggle," originally published in *Cahiers du Cinema*.

PATRICIA GUZMAN, *La insurreccion de la burguesia* (Apartado 14.363 Candelaria. Caracas: Rocimante). 1975. 70 pp.

This book contains the full text of the first section of Guzman's three-part film *La Batalla de Chile*, made with the cooperation of the Cuban Film Institute. The volume also includes the over-all plan of the complete film (three parts, four and one half hours in all), a glossary of *chilenismos* and two reviews of the film.

PATRICIO GUZMAN, *La batalla de Chile: La lucha de un pueblo sin armas*, prologue by Julio Garcia Espinosa and Marta Harnecker, Pamplona, Spain: S. Peralta Ediciones: Libros Hiperion, 1977. Screenplay for Parts I & II of this three-part documentary.

PATRICIO GUZMAN AND PEDRO SEMPERE, *Chile: el cine contra el fascismo*. Valencia, Spain: Fernando Torres, 1977. 250 pp., illus.

Sempere's interview with Patricio Guzman, director of *The Battle of Chile*, comprises half of this book; the remainder consists of collected essays by Latin Americans and Europeans on Guzman's documentaries and miscellaneous materials including portions of the director's shooting diary.

MIGUEL LITTIN, *"El Chacal de Nahueltoro; La tierra prometida,"* UNAM Textos de cine, 5, Serie de guiones, 1. Mexico: D.F. 1977. 134 pp., illus.

A collection of five previously published interviews and articles with/by Miguel Littin, followed by the original treatment for *The Promsed Land*, a short sketch for an unmade film called "La ira acumulada," and, finally, the full screenplay for *The Jackal of Nahueltoro*.

ALICIA VEGA, editor, *Re-vision del cine chileno*, Céntro de Indagacion y Expresion Cultural y Artistica (CENECA). Santiago, Chile: Editorial Aconcagua. 1979. 391 pp., illus.

Prospective filmmakers in Pinochet's Chile, frustrated in their efforts to make films, initiated this research project as a means of recuperating portions of Chilean film history which have been accidentally lost or purposefully destroyed. An "Introduction to the Feature-length Fictional Film" is divided into two parts: Silent Period: 1910-1921, and Sound Period: 1934-1979. Characters, Plot, Dramatic Construction Cinematic Language, Editing and Acting. Included in this selection are Miguel Littin's *The Jackal of Nahueltoro* (1969) and Silvio Caiozzi's *Julio comienza en julio* (Chile, 1979). Patr II is dedicated to documentary films, and Part III to conclusions.

LUIS BOCAZ, editor, "Capitulos de la cultura chilena: El cine," Special section of *Araucaria de Chile* No. 11 (Madrid: Ediciones Michay). 1980, pp. 96-155, illus.

This supplement features interviews with filmmakers Raul Ruiz and Patricio Guzman, a brief essay by Helvio Soto, a roundtable discussion among several leading Chilean writers and filmmakers and a filmography of works produced since the 1973 coup d'etat.

COLOMBIA

HERNANDO MARTÍNEZ PARDO, *Historia del cine colombiano* (Bogotá, Colombia: Editora Guadalupe Ltda.). 1978. 472 pp., illus.

The most complete history of film in Colombia available to date. Organized by periods (1900-1928; 1919-1946; 1947-1960; 1960-1976) the book also includes sections on festivals, film magazines, film societies, and a projection of future prospects.

UMBERTO VALVERDE, *Reportaje critico al cine colombiano* (Bogotá, Colombia: Editorial Toronuevo Limitada). 1978. 355 pp., illus.

A collection of interviews with thirteen leading independent and commercial Colombian filmmakers who came to prominence in the

1960s. Also contains an interview with the leading film society organizer and critic, Hernando Salcedo Silva.

CUBA

Julio Garcia Espinosa, *Por un cine imperfecto* (Selection and Introduction by Edmundo Aray; Apartado 14.363, Candelaria, Caracas: Rocinante). 1973. 69 pp.

A collection of theoretical essays by Cuba's foremost film theorist in addition to the title piece, "For an Imperfect Cinema," more often reprinted than any other essay on Latin American filmmaking, the volume contains "In Search of the Lost Cinema," "Developing a New Culture Over the Dead Body of the Last Members of the Bourgeoisie," and "Intellectuals and Artists of the World, Dis-Unite!"

Gloria Esqueu, compiler, *Indice de la revista Cine cubano, 1960-1974* (Havana: Bibliateca Nacional Jose Marti; Editorial Orbe). 1979, 181 pp.

A very useful index to the most long-lived of the Latin American film journals. Arranged topically, in alphabetical order, with three indices: subject, author, and films cited .

Julio García Espinosa, *Una imagen recorre el mundo* (La Habana, Cuba: Editorial Letras Cubanas). 1979.

A collection of theoretical essays by this filmmaker who is also one of Cuba's leading cultural theorists. The selection includes: "For an Imperfect Cinema," "In Search of the Lost Cinema," "An Image Encircles the Globe," "The Four Communications Media Really Number Only Three: Film and Television," and four others.

DOMINICAN REPUBLIC

Jimmy Sierra, *Cine en Santo Domingo*, Santo Domingo: Comite Pro Instituto Nacional de Estudios Cinematograficos, 1980, 30 pp., illus.

An interview with documentarist Jimmy Sierra by Rafael Portorreal, director of the National Institute of Film Studies.

MEXICO

Miguel Contreras Torres, *El libro negro del cine mexicano* (Mexico: Editora Hispano-Continental Films). 1960. 450 pp.

22

One of Mexico's most prolific producer-directors denounces the monopoly over production and exhibition of William O. Jenkins and his associates. A fascinating view of the Mexican film industry.

EMILIO GARCIA RIERA, *El cine mexicano* (Mexico: Ediciones Era). 1963. 238 pp.
A short, useful history of Mexican filmmaking from its inception through the early 1960s by Mexico's foremost film historian.

FEDERICO HEUER, *La industria cinematografica mexicana* (Mexico: The Author). 1964. 435 pp.
Economic and structural study of the Mexican film industry by a former director of the *Banca Nacional Cinematografica.*

JORGE AYALA BLANCO, *La aventura del cine mexicano* (Aniceto Ortega 1358, Mexico 12, D.F.: Ediciones Era). 1968. 455 pp.
Ayala's ambitious book undertakes to analyze the genesis of Mexican cinema thematically and purports to prove that the Mexican cinema deserves serious consideration apart from the overshadowing creative presence of Luis Bunuel. The last section of this three part study is dedicated to the movement toward a more independent and experimental kind of filmmaking, though the publication date means that the most militant projects are not included.

ALBERTO HIJAR, ed., *Hacia un tercer cine* (Mexico: Direccion General de Difusion Cultural, 10° piso de la Rectoria, Universidad Nacional Autonoma, Mexico 20, D.F., Cuadernos de Cine, No. 20). 1972. 144 pp., illus.
This anthology offers selections from several Latin American film journals, many of which are now unavailable. Despite its loose organization and the unevenness of some of the material, the anthology brings together documentary material from all over Latin America (Brazil, Uruguay, Argentina, Bolivia, Chile and Mexico), and includes such interesting pieces as a reciprocal interview between Argentine director Fernando Solanas and French filmmaker Jean-Luc Godard.

FERNANDO CONTRERAS Y ESPINOSA, *La produccion, sector primario de la industria cinematografica* (Mexico City: UNAM). Textos de Cine 4, 265 pp., illus., tables.
A richly detailed, practical look at the technical aspects of film production in the Mexican film industry.

AURELIO DE LOS REYES, *Los origenes del cine en Mexico: 1896-1900* (Mexico: UNAM. Direccion General de Difusion Cultural) 1973. 196 pp.
A history of the earliest years of Mexican film history.

Jorge Ayala Blanco, *La busqueda del cine mexicano: 1968-1972* (Mexico: UNAM). 1974. 2 vols.

A continuation of his earlier *La aventura del cine mexicano*. Includes a discussion of President Luis Echevarria's attempt to stimulate the industry.

Emilio Garcia Rieta, *Historia documental del cine mexicano* (Mexico: Ediciones Era), 8 volumes, 1969-1974, illus. Vol. 1: 1926-1940, 324 pp.; vol. 2: 1941-1944, 370 pp.; vol. 3: 1945-1948, 370 pp.; vol. 4: 1949-1951, 431 pp.; vol. 5: 1952-1954, 377 pp.; vol. 6: 1955-1957, 385 pp.; vol. 7: 1958-1960, 499 pp.; vol. 8: 1961-1963, 475 pp.

Indispensible reference for serious students of Mexican filmmaking: provides complete credits, production details, synopses and critical commentary on virtually every Mexican film ever made.

PUERTO RICO

El cine visto en Puerto Rico: 1962-1973. Hato Rey: Univ. de Puerto Rico, 1975. 279 pp.

This collection of newspaper articles represent the first attempt to provide an overview of the growth in Puerto Rican film culture over the past decade stimulated mainly by university film societies. A large portion of the book is made up of reviews of foreign films. There is no discussion of incipient Puerto Rican film activity.

VENEZUELA

Vision: Guia venezolana de cine, television, artes escencias y audioxisuales, 1978-1979, 1979-1980. (Apartado 60.844, Chacao, Caracas 106, Venezuela). Illustrated.

A practical guide to the Venezuela film and audi-visual industry.

BOOKS—ENGLISH

GENERAL

CARLOS E. CORTES, LEON G. CAMPBELL AND ALLAN CURL, *A Filmic Approach to the Study of Historical Dilemmas*, Latin American Studies Program Film Series No. 2, October, 1976 (Latin American Studies Program, University of California, Riverside), 47 pp.

LEON G. CAMPBELL AND CARLOS E. CORTES, *Film as Revolutionary Weapon: A Pedagogical Analysis*, Latin American Studies Program Film Series #3 (Latin American Studies Program, University of California, Riverside, 92521), 19 pp.

ALLEN L. WOLL, *The Latin Image in American Film* (Los Angeles: UCLA Latin American Center Publications, 1977), 126 pp.

Disappointedly superficial. A look at how Hollywood has looked at Latin America.

ZUZANA M. PICK, ed., *Latin American Filmmakers and the Third Cinema* (Carleton University Film Studies Program: Ottawa, Canada, 1978), 248 pp.

This anthology, designed as a reader for a Latin American film course, is primarily composed of articles translated from the Cuban film magazine *Cine cubano*. Each of the seven sections is dedicated to a specific country and most often to the work of a single filmmaker of group within that country: Argentina (The *Cine Liberacion* group of Fernando Solanas, Octavio Getino, and Gerardo Vallejo); Bolivia (The Ukamau Group of Jorge Sanjines); Brazil (Glauber Rocha); Chile (Miguel Littin); Colombia (Carlos Alvarez); Uruguay (Mario Handler); and Cuba (various).

The editor sought texts which would "illustrate the filmmakers' search for a theoretical definition of cinema in the context of political change and revolution." Her introduction attempts a critical overview of militant Latin American cinema based on Fernando Solanas' and Octavio Getino's concept of "Third Cinema," though the author declares in her final paragraph that "Today, the Third Cinema is dead and only through its study by critics and historians will it contribute to the creation of a new cinema aesthetic."

Despite the unevenness of the introduction, the imperfection of some of the translations, and the inevitable exclusivity of a limited number of selections, this volume fills a long-standing gap and performs a great service to English-speaking audiences of Latin American film.

CARLOS E. CORTES AND LEON G. CAMPBELL, *Race and Ethnicity in the Americas: A Filmic Approach*, Latin American Studies Program Film Series No. 4 (Latin American Studies Program, University of California, Riverside, 92521), 1979, 56 pp.

The fourth in a series, this booklet, like its predecessors, synthesizes the experience of a particular film and history course. The introduction offers basic bibliography related to the concepts of race and ethnicity in the Americas, as well as a description of the focus and pedagogical philosophy of the course. The bulk of the pamphlet consists of fourteen brief student essays, generally comparative, on films from Latin America and elsewhere.

BRAZIL

JOHNSON, RANDAL AND ROBERT STAM, eds., *Brazilian Cinema* (East New Brunswick, New Jersey: Associated University Presses). 1982. 373 pp., illus.

An essential collection of reprinted and original articles by Brazilian nationals as well as foreign scholars. Includes critical essays on specific films as well as more historical and thematic articles.

CHILE

MICHAEL CHANAN, *Chilean cinema*(London: British Film Institute). 1976. 102 pp.

Interviews reprinted from *Cahiers du Cinema* and other European sources with directors Raul Ruiz, Helvio Soto and Miguel Littin and communications theorist Armand Mattelart are followed by reprints of several brief articles in the British, U.S. and Chilean press, a filmography and bibliography. The selection is an interesting one, and the editor's excellent introduction places the entire volume in a necessarily broad perspective.

CUBA

MICHAEL MYERSON, *Memories of Underdevelopment: The Revolutionary Films of Cuba* (New York: Grossman). 1973. 303 pp., illus.

A reconstruction (on the basis of the English subtitles and sometimes faulty observation) of the script of Gutierrez Alea's *Memories of Underdevelopment* and of the third episode of Humberto Solas' *Lucia.* Also includes a summary of other Cuban films and an introduction by the author which, if not as direct and informative as one might hope on the topic of Cuban filmmaking, does provide an excellent account of the aborted attempt to organize a festival of Cuban films in New York in 1972.

MICHAEL CHANAN, editor, *DFI Dossier #2: Santiago Alvarez* (London: British Film Iistitute). 1980. 71 pp., illus.

Compiled "to accompany the most complete retrospective of Alvarez' work yet seen outside Cuba" (London, spring 1980), the collection contains an introduction in Chanan's characteristically meditative style, followed by Derek Malcolm's dense and eloquent "master of the Moviola," a translation of "From Hanoi to Yungay," Miguel Orodea's fascinating comparison of "Alvarez and Vertov" and Alvarez' own "Cinema as one of the Mass Communications Media." In Chanan's "Annotated Filmography" which comprises the second half of the volume, commentaries on Alvarez' films from 1960 through 1979 range from a scant two lines to four full pages. A fundamental source for the study of this foremost Cuban documentarist.

MEXICO

BEATRIZ REYES NEVARES, *The Mexican Cinema: Interviews with Thirteen Directors* (Albuquerque: University of New Mexico Press). 1976. Illus.

A Mexican journalist and critic interviews Mexico's film pioneers and young crusaders, including Luis Bunuel, Emilio "El Indio" Fernandez, Luis Alcoriza, Felipe Cazals, Arturo Ripstein and Sergio Olhovich. Unfortunately, the interviews appear to have been conducted without benefit of historical or critical background in film on the part of the interviewer.

ARTHUR G. PETTIT, *Images of the Mexican American in Fiction and Film* (Texas A&M University Press: College Station). 282 pp., illus.

(Unable to examine by press date.)

ARTICLES

GENERAL

JOHN GILLET, "South of the Border," *Sight and Sound*, Autumn, 1960, pp. 188-191, illus.

Instructive as a preface to the New Latin American cinema which would subsequently develop, this early piece summarizes and generally deplores the sporadic offerings from Argentina, Mexico and Brazil available in Europe in the late 1950s. Though the author's attempts to explain the stasis are totally unsatisfactory, the subsequent decade provided overwhelming vindication for his closing words: "Many of the cinema's best artists have been rebels and renegades of a kind; and in their present state of development, the cinemas of South and Central America seem to need all the rebels they can find. Time, though, is on their side."

"Walter Achugar on Latin American Cinema," *Cineaste*, Vol. IV, No. 3, Winter 1970-71, pp. 35 and 52.

Achugar, head of Uruguay's Third World Cinematheque, and a major force behind the scenes of militant Latin American filmmaking, gives a brief overview of the situation in Argentina, Bolivia, Chile and Uruguay in 1969 and 1970, including the history of the Cinematheque.

DAVID WILSON, "Aspects of Latin American Political Cinema," *Sight and Sound*, Vol. 41, No. 3, Summer, 1972, pp. 127-131, illus.

After an introductory section which asserts the ideological nature of all film products and the structurally predetermined inefficacy of most "so-called political cinema," Wilson launches into a perceptive and informative discussion of the theory and practice of the Latin American militant cinema, placing special emphasis on the ideas of Fernando Solanas and Octavio Getino (*The Hour of the Furnaces*). Wary of appearing to postulate any single theoretical position as universally valid in the highly diversified Latin American context, Wilson turns instead to the more general task of examining thematic similarities and divergences in several films. Among those he singles out are: affirmation of national identity in the face of underdevelopment and concomitant economic and ideological dependency; cultural alienation and the need for cultural decolonization; the power of myth and superstition in popular life; the need for organized and violent collective action.

This serious, informative and intelligent article takes the British National Film Theatre's festival of Latin American political cinema as its point of departure, discussing films from Brazil, Chile, Bolivia, Colombia, Mexico and Cuba, and returning to the Argentine documentary *The Hour of the Furnaces* as a kind of leitmotif.

E. BRADFORD BURNS, "The Latin American Film, Realism and the Historian," *The History Teacher*, Vol. VI, No. 4, August, 1973, pp. 569-574.

The development of indigenous filmmaking with an eye to the anlysis and transformation of national reality is summarized by Burns in an appeal to Latin American historians to take advantage of these valuable "film-texts" whose realism consists in "documenting the frustrations, discontent and longing for change characteristic of modern Latin America" and in "virtually recreating the events of the past."

CONCETTA CARESTIA GREENWOOD, "The New South American Cinema: From Neo-Realism to Expressive Realism," *Latin American LIbrary Review*, Vol. 1, No. 2, spring, 1973, pp. 111-123.

This article draws from a number of films and critical essays in order to "clarify the major ideological and aesthetic connotations of the New [Latin American] cinema, its themes and its styles," emphasizing "the major statement" of the Brazilian Cinema Novo. The author discusses *The Hour of the Furnaces* in some detail, *The Jackal of Nahueltoro* and *Blood of the Condor* very briefly, but devotes most of her energy to the "stylistic perfection" and mythical-mystical trappings of Glauber Rocha's *Antonio das Mortes*. Minor factual errors (Bertolucci as director of *The Battle of Algiers*) combined with a certain narrowness of conception ("expressive realism") becomes too vague a term when applied to all the approaches taken by the New Latin American filmmakers; other film movements are bound to be misunderstood if they are exclusively viewed as deriving from or aspiring to Brazilian Cinema Novo) limit the article's value.

GARY CROWDUS, "The Montreal 'New Cinema' Conference," *Cineaste*, Vol. VI, No. 3, fall, 1974, pp. 26-28. Illus.

An account of the *Recontres Internationales Pour un Nouveau Cinema* (June 2-8, 1974) which recapitulates the general lines of debate involving Fernando Solanas from Argentina (on Peronism) and Cuba's Julio Garcia Espinosa (on revolutionary film form), among others.

AMOS VOGEL, *Film as a Subversive Art* (New York: Random House, 1974). "The Third World: A New Cinema," pp. 159-168. Illus.

29

A brief selection, studded with illustrations, which alludes to films from Cuba, Brazil, Mexico and Argentina, among others. The short scope necessitates superficiality.

JULIANNE BURTON, "Learning to Write at the Movies: Film and the Fiction Writer in Latin America," *The Texas Quarterly* (Austin), Vol. 27, No. 1 (spring, 1975), pp. 92-103.

Argues that the formation of the contemporary Latin American writer, once the product of primarily literary influences, is now increasingly cinematic. Discusses the cases of Guillermo Cabrera Infante, Carlos Fuentes, Manuel Puig and Gabriel Garcia Marquez in particular.

JULIANNE BURTON, "The Old and the New: Latin American Cinema at the (Last?) Pesaro Festival," *Jump/Cut*, No. 9, October-December, 1975, pp. 33-35.

A summary of the 11th Mostra Internazionale del Nuovo Cinema at Pesaro, Italy, from September 8th to 14th, 1975, which details two of the festival's three areas of emphasis: the retrospective of Brazil's Cinema Novo movement, and the most recent Latin American film production.

SUSAN TARR AND HANS PROPPE, "The Cinema of Conspicuous Production," *Towards Revolutionary Art*, Vol. 2, No. 2, 1975, pp. 8-17. Illus.

Largely an adaptation of Argentine director Fernando Solanas' ideas on "First Cinema" (bourgeois, Hollywood film production) as put forth in "Towards a Third Cinema." In the interest of "clarifying, demystifying and making more accessible the political uses of film," and using Latin American militant filmmaking as a case in point, the authors begin with a classification and critique of existing books on film and proceed to make a case for the political nature of all art. The characteristics and effects of "first cinema" are juxtaposed to some insufficiently elaborated examples of recent Latin American films.

PETER BISKIND, "In Latin America they shoot filmmakers," *Sight and Sound* (London), 45. Summer, 1976, pp. 160-161.

On official repression against filmmakers in Chile, Bolivia and Argentina.

JULIANNE BURTON, "The Hour of the Embers: On the Current Situation of Latin American Cinema," *Film Quarterly*, Vol. XXX, No. 1, Fall, 1976, pp. 33-44, illus.

An assessment of the situation for filmmakers in Colombia, Ecuador, Peru, Argentina, Brazil and Venezuela in the mid-seventies, with summaries of key films.

LEONARDO LUXEMBURG, "Latin American Films: Fourth Frontier," in Jean Marie Ackerman, ed., *Films of a Changing Worlds A Critical International Guide*, Vol. II, Washington, D.C.: Society for International Development, 1977, pp. 34-36, illus.

A brief, superficial and relatively early article which provides cursory appraisals of *Memories of Underdevelopment, Lucia, The Hour of the Furnaces* and *The Jackal of Nahueltoro*.

JULIANNE BURTON, "The Camera as 'Gun': Two Decades of Film Culture and Resistance in Latin America," *Latin American Perspectives*, Vol. V, No. 1 (Issue 16), Winter, 1978, pp. 49-76, illus.

A critical history of militant political cinema movements or form of political and cultural resistance in Brazil, Argentina, Bolivia, Colombia, Peru and Chile from the late 1950's through the late 1970s.

JOHN MOSIER, "Currents in Latin American Film," *Americas*, Vol. 30, No. 5, May, 1978, pp. 2-8, illus.

This nicely illustrated article maintains that despite stylistic and formal differences, Latin American films demonstrate a basic unity in their thematic preocupation with "the ordeal of autonomy." "The real genius of Latin American film," the author maintains, "has been to place fundamental moral and behavioral issues in the context of extensive social and political themes."

After a capsule history of the evolution of the film medium in Latin America in the context of world film history, Mosier selects several films of the 1960s and 1970s to illustrate his thesis. The utility of the piece is diminished by a diffuse analytical framework and the author's apparent obliviousness to the numerous political and aesthetic indicators which from the mid-seventies have pointed to an impending crisis.

ERDMUNTE WENZEL WHITE, "A Movie Is What Is Left of the Looking: Latin American Cinema, Its Contribution to Revolutionary Film Language," *1978 Film Studies Annual* (Purdue University), pp. 18-20.

The ambitious title promises much more than this brief, equivocal essay delivers. A minor meditation on the potential coincidence of political and aesthetic vanguardism in Latin American film, this piece demonstrates little effort to address the important question it raises, preferring instead to take refuge behind an inconclusive and arbitrary montage of quotes from other writers.

ANNETTE TRAVERSIE BAGLEY AND BRUCE M. BAGLEY, "Film and Society: A Survey of Latin American Political Cinema," *American Film Institute Education Newsleter,t* Vol. 3, No. 2, November-December, 1979 (no page numbers).

Thumbnail sketches of filmmaking activity in Brazil, Cuba, Argentina, Chile and Bolivia and a list of general readings are followed by descriptions of selected films from each country and brief national bibliographies. Remarkably tight and complete, given the necessarily limited scope of the format. Succeeds admirably in its goal of offering an outline and list of filmic and critical texts for a course on Latin American film.

DANIEL I. GEFFNER, "Film and Revolution in Latin America: Conceptualizing a Structural Framework for an 'Engaged Cinema,'" *Proceedings of the Pacific Coast Council on Latin American Studies*, Vol. 6, 1977-79, pp. 231-47.

This essay begins with a discussion of the discrepancies between approaches to revolutionary cinema in Europe and in the Third World, and goes on to propose "a structural framework within which to analyze revolutionary films" which consists of three interrelated categories: "textual" ("encompassing the many factors which make up content and form"), and "processual" (processes by which the film is to be produced"), and "conditional" ("all those factors affecting the film over which the artists have no control"). Prominent films and filmmakers are used to illustrate each of these categories. Though uneven at times, this ambitious article is serious and suggestive.

PAUL J. VANDERWOOD, 'Response to 'Film and Revolution in Latin America,'" *Proceedings of the Pacific Coast Council on Latin American Studies*, Vol. 6, 1977-79, pp. 248-52.

In response to Daniel Geffner's attempt to formulate a theoretical/methodological framework in which to understand revolutionary film practice in Latin American (see G. Gedney listing). Vanderwood raises a number of omitted issues and challenges several fundamental assumptions. Clearfly the product of his own unresolved reflections, his queries are both sincere and suggestive.

MICHAEL CHANAN, "Latin American Film Festival in Havana," *Framework: A Film Journal*, No. 2, pp. 37-40, illus.

This report on the First International Festival of the New Latin American Cinema (Havana, December 1979) focuses on a tiny selection of the more than 300 documentary and fictional films shown. It includes a brief discussion of the symposium on the multiational mass culture industry, and concludes with an interesting attempt to generalize common elements (constant mobility of the camera, syncopated cutting, insistence on political signification through montage) amid heterogeneous approaches, themes and styles.

LYNN GARAFOLA, "The New Latin American Cinema and Cuba," *Socialist Review*, Vol. 10, No. 4, July-August, 1980, pp. 130-135.

This report on the First International Festival of the New Latin American Cinema, held in Havana in December of 1979, offers brief assessments of a number of notable films. Choosing Cuba, Venezuela, Nicaragua and the Chicano filmmakers as the most important national groupings, the author isolates several themes which characterize the Latin American film ouput: "If national affirmation, often coupled with anti-imperialism, was the official themes of the Festival, race and feminism were its unacknowledged leit-motifs."

JASON JOHANSEN, "A New Wave Cresting," *Nuestro*, May, 1980, pp. 24-25, 63, illus.

Briefly surveys film production in four Latin American countries: Chile, Panama, Nicaragua, and Cuba identified as "the creative center" of the New Latin American Cinema movement.

ALBERT JOHNSON, "Albert Johnson from Havana," *Film Comment*, Vol. 16, No. 3, May-June, 1980, pp. 2, 4.

This report of the First International Festival of the New Latin American Cinema (Havana, December, 1979), is of limited usefulness because of its cursory scope and frequent errors.

JOHN MOSIER, "The First Latin American Film Festival," *New Orleans Review*, Vol. 7, No. 2 (Summer, 1980), pp. 195-197.

This account of the first *international* Latin American film festival (Havana, December 1979), commends the Cubans on the organization and execution of the festival itself while at the same time lambasting Cuban cinema for having "run out of gas," for being unable to "raise up anyone comparable in talent" to Tomas Gutierrez Alea, who got his training as a filmmaker prior to the revolution and hence "learned how to make movies on his own, and for 'overpowering sense of grayness that . . . is . . . only an image of an increasingly gray society.' "

JOHN MOSIER, "Latin American Cinema in the Seventies," *New Orleans Review*, Vol. 7, No. 3 (Fall, 1980), pp. 229-236, illus.

Criticizing the "surprisingly rigid critical posture" of commentators who mourn the demise of the New Latin American Cinema, the author assesses the seventies in Latin American film industries as "a moving . . . towards a gentler, more genuinely cinematic" style and a "shaking out of talent." His account centers on activity in Cuba and Brazil, with emphasis on the latter because "Despite the more widely reported attempts of the Cubans, the real developmental model . . . has occurred in Brazil during the seventies." Mexico, Chile and Brazil also receive passing attention in what the author admits is a very broad and general account of a decade of developments in the Latin American film sector.

ZUZANA M. PICK, "The Cinema of Latin America: A Constantly Changing Problematic," *Cine-tracts*, Vol. 3, No. 1 (Winter, 1980), pp. 50-55.

This final segment of a special dossier on Chilean cinema branches out to assess the limitations of the Mexican film industry and the Brazilian Cinema Novo movement and, turning for support to Cuban filmmaker-theorist Julio Garcia Espinosa, Colombian Carlos Alvarez and Bolivian Jorge Sanjines, states the need for a more theoretical understanding of three interlated issues: cultural colonialism, public taste, and popular cinema.

ARGENTINA—(General)

E. BRADFORD BURNS, "National Identity in Argentine Films," *Americas*, Vol. 27, Nos. 11-12, November-December, 1975, pp. 4-10, illus.

An excellent and generously illustrated general introduction to early Argentine cinema (1897 through the 1930s) which focuses on film as an agent in the formation of national identity—from the valiant rural gaucho to the plaintive city-dwelling singer of tangos.

JORGE MIGUEL COUSELO, "The Connection: Three Essays on the Treatment of History in the Early Argentine Cinema" (translated and introduced by E. Bradford Burns, University of California, Los Angeles), *Journal of Latin American Lore*, Vol. 1, No. 2, 1975, pp. 211-230.

These three essays, originally published in an Argentine historical journal, each assemble all available data on early (1916-1972) Argentine independent film and the "pioneer" responsible for it. The first essay and the third ("*Mariano Moreno*: An Early Historical Film") and "Clemente Onelli and the Pedagogic Values of Film") are of limited interest, but the second article, "*The Last Indian Rebellion*: An Anthro-Historical Film," provides a fascinating account of an extraordinary early feature which anticipates numerous film practices that, in the late 1960s, would come to characterize the New Latin American cinema, e.g., the mixtures of fictional and documentary modalities, the use of non-professional actors to reconstruct historical events based on their own experience, the self-reflexive incorporation of the filmmaker himself into the work. This account of Alcides Greca's *El ultimo malon* (1917) is a major contribution to the history of filmmaking in Latin America, and the mention of Fernando Birri's revival of the film in 1956 at his newly founded Institute of Documentary Film in Santa Fe establishes a direct link between this early landmark "fictional documentary" and the subsequent evolution of the New Latin American Cinema movement.

34

STEVE KOVACS, "Screening the Movies in Argentina," *New Boston Review*, Vol. 111, No. III (December, 1977), pp. 19-21.

An informative overview of Argentine film activity from 1973 to 1976, an important historical period which the author calls "this nation's second rendez-vous with Juan Domingo Peron." Based on personal interviews, Kovacs' account focuses on the issue of censorship, first under the stewardship of left-wing Peronist Octavio Getino (co-director of *The Hour of the Furnaces*), then, after the military coup which outsted Peron's widow, on the pious, paternalistic, and proto-fascist practices of Miguel Paulino Tato.

ARGENTINA—(Eduardo de Gregorio)

JIM HILLER AND TOM MILNE, "Out of the Past: An Interview with Eduardo de Gregorio," *Sight and Sound*, Vol. 49, No. 2, Spring, 1980, pp. 91-95, illus.

Screenwriter and filmmaker Eduardo de Gregorio, who "left Argentina at the end of 1966 because I wanted to make movies and that had become almost impossible [there]," now lives in Paris. In this interview he discusses his collaboration with Bernardo Bertolucci (*The Spider's Strategem*), Jacques Rivette (*Celine and Julie Go Boating*), and Jean-Louis Comolli (*La Cecilia*) as well as two feature films of his own (*Serail*, 1975, and *La Memoire Courte*, 1979). In his account of himself as an Argentine-bred cineaste in Paris, de Gregorio also reflects upon the rise of neo-Fascism in Europe, the impact of writer Jorge Luis Borges, the problematicity of the concept of "cultural decolonization" in Argentina, and the bankruptcy of *la politique des auteurs* in contemporary France.

ARGENTINA—(Raymundo Gleyer)

MARK FALCOFF, "Original Sin and Argentine Reality: Peronist History and Myth in THE TRAITORS," *Proceeding of the Pacific Coast Council on Latin American Studies*, Vol. 6, 1977-79, pp. 217-30.

An impressive analysis of this clandestine feature, considered by the author to be "the finest of all Argentine political films, and very possibly one of the finest political films ever made anywhere." Falcoff begins with an historical interpretation of the unlikely "wedding" of Peronism and militant cinema, starting with Solanas' and Getino's *The Hour of the Furnaces*, and contextualizes the production of *The Traitors* as spanning "roughly the months between the inauguration of Hector

Campora and the commencement of Peron's third presidency on 12 October 1973." Part II offers a plot summary, exemplary in both its detail and its accuracy. Part III assesses the artistic qualities of the film while Parts IV and V analyze the ideological intricacies of a feature which, in the author's opinion, "fails as political propaganda [—but] succeeds as cineastic art."

ARGENTINA—(Jorge Preloran)

HOWARD SURER, "Porge Prelorán: An Interview," *Film Comment* (Spring, 1971), pp. 43-51.

This prolific ethnographic documentarist discusses his method and his films.

ARGENTINA—(Fernando Solanas and Octavio Getino)

"Cinema as a Gun: An Interview with Fernando Solanas" (translated from *Ombre Rosse* by Rebecca Douglass), *Cineaste*, Vol. III, No. 2, Fall, 1969, pp. 18-26, illus.

An important early interview with the co-director of *The Hour of the Furnaces* upon the European premiere of his film at Pesaro. Solanas details briefly the historical, political and cinematic genesis of the film and discusses each of the three parts as well as the obstacles to the distribution and the solutions developed by the filmmakers.

JAMES ROY MACBEAN, "La Hora de los Hornos," *Film Quarterly*, Vol. 24, No. 1, fall, 1970, pp. 31-37. (Reprinted in MacBean's *Film and Revolution*, Bloomington: Indiana University Press, 1975.)

Faced with the difficulty of "hazarding an appraisal" of the aesthetic results of a film whose aesthetics and politics are so inextricably intertwined, the author concentrates on the stylistic and thematic variations of this four-and-a-half-hour "film mosaic," recapitulating each of its three parts in its virtuoso juxtaposition of so many different styles and contests, since the result succeeds in conveying the complexity of the Argentine situation.

"Fernando Solanas: An Interview" (translated from *Cinethique* by James Roy MacBean), *Film Quarterly*, Vol. 24, No. 2, Winter, 1970-71, pp. 37-43.

Fernando Solanas discusses how the *Grupo Cine Liberacion* transformed the process of film production in order to produce *The Hour of the Furnaces,* asserting that filmmakers have to become skilled in and responsible for every segment of production and distribution in order to free themselves from a capitalist dominated system. Solanas compares the strengths of the fictional and documentary forms and the revolutionary potential of each, and discusses the search for a "revolutionary" film language in a neocolonial situation.

JOEL HAYCOCK, "Notes on Solanas and Godard," *Rilm Society Review,* Vol. 7, No. 3, November, 1971, pp. 30-31, and Vol. 7, No. 4, December, 1971, pp. 31-36. Revised and reprinted from *Camera People,* summer, 1971.) Illus.

Haycock's two-part article contrasts the technique of four post-May '68 films by Godard and his Dziga Vertov group (*Un Film Comme les Lautres, See You at Mao, Pravda,* and *Vent D'est*) with those used by Solanas in *The Hour of the Furnaces.* His thesis is that despite the affinities of the two directors, Solanas' film (because it lacks the constant self-reflectiveness of the Godard films mentioned) cannot serve as a model for political cinema in the developed world, where the first priority is to expose the ideological dimension of all images and presentations. Because Solanas obviously believes in the truth of the objects and phenomena which his camera converts into images, Haycock accuses him of developing "a radical film grammar" which is ultimately "petit-bourgeois" in essence and as such not applicable to the "neo-capitalist" world. Some confused political preconceptions cloud and cast doubt upon his argument.

LOUIS MARCORELLES, "Solanas: Film as a Political Essay" (translated from *Cahiers du Cinema* by Helen R. Lane), *Evergreen,* July 1969, pp. 31-33.

A solemn yet enthusiastic response to the Pesaro screening of *The Hour of the Furnaces* which situates that open-ended film essay in the context of world film history and calls it "probably the greatest historical film ever made."

JOHN MATTHEWS, ". . . And After?: A Response to Solanas and Getino," *Afterimage,* No. 3, Summer, 1971, pp. 36-39.

The author tries to set Solanas' and Getino's film and theoretical-practical declaration into a framework of European theories of ideology and First World film practice. In his view, Solanas' and Getino's importance lies in their emphasis on transforming the means of cinematic production and distribution, but he feels that "a contradiction in media" makes this only truly feasible in video. Matthews also tries to come to grips with the paradox of First World acclaim for these Third World filmmakers whose goal is that their work remain indigestible in the metropolitan realm.

OCTAVIO GETINO AND FERNANDO SOLANAS, "Towards a Third Cinema" (translated from *Tricontinental*, OSPAAL, 1969), *Afterimage*, No. 3, Summer, 1971, pp. 16-35, illus. Also in *Cineaste*, Vol. IV, No. 3, Winter, 1970-71, pp. 1-10, illus.

Still perhaps the most seminal theoretical manifesto to come out of the New Latin American Cinema movement, this article identifies cinematographic militancy as a product of changing historical conditions from Vietnam to Latin America and postulates a new decolonizing conception of art, and a new approach to culture in general and filmmaking in particular. Solanas and Getino discuss commercial cinematic forms as generators and reflectors of bourgeois, consumer-oriented ideology and posit "Third Cinema" as an alternative to both the Hollywood-style commercial film style and the European concept of a *"cinema des auteurs."* The authors offer a blueprint for this guerrilla cinema based on their experience with *The Hour of the Furnaces.*

DAN RANVAUD, "Fernando Solanas: An Interview," *Framework: A Film Journal*, No. 10 (Spring, 1979), pp. 35-58, illus.

A shaggy, run-on interview with the co-director of the landmark Argentine documentary *The Hour of the Furnaces*, about his subsequent feature *The Sons of Martin Fierro*. Solanas repeats his case in defense of Peron, denounces "the universal institutionalized communist structure" in its complicity with the "neo-colonial apparatus," describes his film as the cornerstone of a new epic-political-poetic genre (a "cinema of argumental vicissitudes"!) and casts himself as "part of the collective memory of the people without the constraints of the intellectual elites." Lazy editing and over-literal translations do little to soften the grating edge of Solanas' personality that comes across in this interview.

FERNANDO SOLANAS, Bertrand Tavernier, Rene Vautier, Guy Hennebelle, "The Cinema: Art Form or Political Weapon," *Framework: A Film Journal*, No. 11 (Autumn, 1979), pp. 10-15, illus.

A discussion/debate on the form and politics of "progressive cinema" which takes Solanas' *The Hour of the Furnaces* as its point of departure and in which Solanas sets forth three levels of critical inquiry and "clarifies" (reformulates) his and Octavio Getino's concept of "First," "Second," and "Third Cinema." Other topics of discussion include the internal hegemony of American movies, film as a vehicle for the expression of "personal" or "collective" mythologies, and outlets for working class expression.

ROBERT STAM, *"Hour of the Furnaces* and the Two Avant Gardes," *Millenium Film Journal*, pp. 151-164, illus.

In this lucid and literate anlysis of *The Hour of the Furnaces* as "one of the high points of convergence" between the formal and the theoretico-political avant-gardes, Stam presents his readers with a high-point in the equally rare convergence of formally sophisticated and politically informed criticism. His comprehensive analysis encompasses the process of production and the "radical interventionism" of the various textual and extra-textual strategies the film adopts to turn passive consumers into active accomplices. Equipped as he is with "the luxury of retrospective lucidity," Stam's criticism of the film's weaknesses are just as illuminating as his appraisal of its strengths. Prior attempts to deal critically with this landmark documentary pale in in comparison with this superlative analysis.

BOLIVIA—(Antonio Eguino)

ERICH KEEL, "From Militant Cinema to Neorealism: The Example of *Pueblo Chico*," *Film Quarterly*, Vol. 19, No. 4 (Summer, 1976), pp. 17-24, illus.

A description and analysis of the first feature film made jointly by Antonio Eguino and Oscar Soria, former members of Jorge Sanjines' *Grupo Ukamau* who remained in Bolivia after a 1971 coup d'etat which made Sanjines and Ricardo Rada, the two other mambers of the original group, *de facto* exiles. This more "pragmatic" film, which "decided to trade ideological correctness and clarity for survival" is contrasted to the group's earlier, more militant (and "manipulative") practice. Parallels with the situation and methodology of Italian filmmakers in the mid and late forties are set forth at length. The essay would have benefitted from a more careful distinction between realist and "neorealist" film, and from an exploration of the rich heritage of both in Latin American film prior to *Pueblo Chico*. The interest and usefulness of Kael's piece has been enhanced by the critical success in this country of Eguino's and Soria's subsequent feature, *Chuquiago* (1978).

JULIANNE BURTON, "*Chuquiago* (The Unspoken and the Unspeakable)," *Cineaste*, Vol. 9, No. 3, Spring, 1979, pp. 50-53, illus.

A consideration of Eguino's and Soria's "return to Neo-realism" as an ideological and political retreat, based on a reading of *Chuquiago* which argues that it successfully reinscribes itself into the very system it purports to critize, ultimately enhancing the mythical invulnerability of that system,'" due to its ahistoricism and failure to articulate social interrelationships.

UDAYAN GUPTA, "Neo-Realism in Bolivia: An Interview with Antonio Eguino," *Cineaste*, Vol. 9, No. 2, Winter, 1978-79, pp. 26-29, 59, illus.

Antonio Eguino, cameraman on Sanjines' *Blood of the Condor*

(1969) and *The Courage of the People* (1971), and later director of *Pueblo Chico* (1974) and *Chuquiago* (1978), discusses these four films and proposes a "new" direction for Latin American filmmaking—"social, analytical films, not radical ones as before."

ALFONSO GUMUCIO DAGRON, *"Chuquiago*: X-Ray of a City" (translated by Dan Wohlfeiler and Julianne Burton), *Jump/Cut: A Review of Contemporary Cinema*, No. 23 ,October, 1980, pp. 6-8, illus.

A serious and suggestive assessment of this important Bolivian feature (the most popular in the country's history) from within its own national context, by a leading Bolivian filmmaker-critic, which ends with a deliberation on the various paths open to filmmaking in Bolivia at the present juncture.

BOLIVIA—(Jorge Sanjines)

"UKAMAU AND YAWAR MALLKU: An Interview with Jorge Sanjines," *Afterimage*, No. 3, Summer, 1971, pp. 40-53, illus.

Sanjines answers basic questions about his early training and his first two feature films, *Ukamau* (1966) and *Yawar Mallku* [*Blood of the Condor*] (1968).

GIBRIL BALDE, BLOOD OF THE CONDOR: "A Talk with Jorge Sanjines"; "BLOOD OF THE CONDOR and the Rats"; and Jorge Sanjines, "Cinema and Revolution, *Cineaste*, Vol. IV, No. 3, Winter, 1970-71, pp. 11-14, illus.

This series of early short pieces by Sanjines and/or about *Blood of the Condor* underline the interest with which this film was received at home and abroad. (Reprints of the first two pieces also appear in *Atlas*, Vol. 20, No. 4, April 1971, pp. 47-48 and 50.)

"THE COURAGE OF THE PEOPLE: An Interview with Jorge Sanjines" (translated from the Uruguyan weekly, *Marcha*, by Rafael Cook), *Cineaste*, Vol. V, No. 2, Spring, 1972, pp. 18-20, illus.

The director *of Blood of the Condor* discusses his subsequent film as a "quest for a people's cinema—in the sense that participation by the people and communication with the people give to the term." Abandoning the fictional mode of the earlier film, *The Courage of the People* offers an historical reconstruction of a government massacre of miners in 1967, with a cast of "re-protagonists" (actual survivors of the event) rather than actors. Sanjines concludes: "We are no longer interested in film that merely invokes and represents the people, but rather in the experience of film that is made from inside the people...who have lived their history."

MICHAEL SHEDIN, "Case Study vs. Process Study: Two Films Made for Italian Television," *Film Quarterly*, Vol. XXVII, No. 3, Spring, 1974, pp. 27-39, illus.

A comparison of Paolo and Vittorio Taviani's *San Michele Had a Rooster* and Sanjines' *The Night of San Juan* (*The Courage of the People*), both financed by Radiotelevisione Italiana. The article compares Sanjines' "objective," historical reconstruction approach with the Taviani's "subjective" fictional mode as two contrasting approaches to political filmmaking. Shedlin asserts, that the Tavianis' film ("case study" or "intellectual',) is made for those already committed, whereas Sanjines' film ("process study" or "propaganda") aims at a cinema *with* and *for* the masses," avoiding "psychological contradictions and theoretical abstractions" to deal concretely with day-to-day experience and the means of throwing off oppression. His detailed attention to the Italian film and the comparative short shrift given the Bolivian production reveal a certain bias, but the end of the article opts for a rather unconvincing reconciliation of the two: "The diversity of the modern radical cinema is its healthiest characteristic....All movies are significant."

LEON G. CAMPBELL AND CARLOS E. CORTES, "Film as a Revolutionary weapon: A Jorge Sanjines Retrospective," *The History Teacher*, Vol. 12, No. 3, May, 1979, pp. 383-402.

An inquiry into the context, content, methodology, target audience and impact of the evolving film practice of Jorge Sanjines and the Ukamau Group, focusing primarily on *Blood of the Condor* (1969) and *The Principal Enemy* (1974). Time has subsequently made clear that group members Antonio Eguino and Oscar Soria have chosen to work independently of Sanjines with a different methodology and set of goals, creating a second "Grupo Ukamau" whose films *Pueblo Chico* and *Chuquiago* should not be considered in an evaluation of Sanjines.

LEON G. CAMPBELL AND CARLOS E. CORTES, "Jorge Sanjines: A Filmic Biography," *Proceedings of the Pacific Coast Council on Latin American Studies*, Vol. 6, 1977-1979, pp. 253-258.

A useful overview of the evolution and contributions of this Bolivian filmmaker, founder of the *Grupo Ukamau*, from his early filmic education through *The Principal Enemy* (1974), made in Peru after he was denied re-entry into Bolivia.

JORGE SANJINES, "Language and Popular Culture," translated by John King, *Framework: A Film Journal*, No. 10, spring, 1979, pp. 31-33, illus.

41

An important piece in which the Bolivian filmmaker synthesizes the formal and methodological evolution of the Ukamau Group based on their commitment to historical reconstruction, actor-participants, collective protagonists, long shots and long takes, and the filmmaker as "the instrument of expression of the community." *The Courage of the People*, *The Principal Enemy* and *Fuera de aquí!* (Get Out of Here!) are discussed in some detail.

BRAZIL—(General)

ALEX VIANY, "Brazil: In Step with a Latin Beat," *Films and Filming*, Vol. X, No. 2, November, 1963, pp. 51-54, illus.

A comprehensive appraisal of the Cinema Novo movement in 1963, virtually at the moment of its inception. Though the author's reasons for characterizing this cinematic flowering as "natural and inevitable" are over-vague, his flashback history of the film medium in Brazil from 1898 and his intelligent reappraisal of the generally scorned *chanchada* genre (slapdash musical farce) are very valuable. Viany conveys the critical and theoretical scope of the movement through well-chosen quotations from the emerging filmmakers: Carlos Diegues, Marcos Farias, Eduardo Coutinho, the late Miguel Torres, Nelson Pereira dos Santos, and the inevitable Glauber Rocha.

RUI NOGUEIRRA AND NICOLETTA ZALAFFI, "Brasil Ano 1970: Round Table on the Cinema Novo," *Cinema*, No. 5, February, 1970, pp. 15-20, illus.

Glauber Rocha, first spokesperson of the Cinema Novo, discusses the origins, development and current situation of the movement with three younger directors (Neville d'Almeida, Julio Bressane and Mauricio Gomes Leite) and producer Jose Leite Viana. Among specific topics are a defense of Brazil's "democratic" censors (it seems that their democracy consists in their arbitrariness) and of music as Brazil's quintessential cultural expression. Rocha, always somewhat of an intellectual pendulum, is here at one of his more obtuse and misleading extremes.

ALEX VIANY, "The Old and the New in Brazilian Cinema," *The Drama Review*, Vol. 14, No. 2, Winter, 1970, pp. 141-144, illus.

A superficial and disjointed survey of Brazilian cinema preceding and during the first few years of Cinema Novo by a noted Brazilian film critic.

LEIF FURHAMMAR AND FOLKE ISAKSSON, "Cinema Novo: Brazil Before the Revolution," *Politics and Film* (New York: Praeger, 1971).

An unexceptional account of selected films from the early and middle periods of Cinema Novo which, due to the early date of its writing, essentially misconstrues the motives and intentions of Brazil's military government vis-a-vis the Cinema Novo movement, giving the junta more credit than is its due.

JAIME RODRIGUES, "Brazil 1970: A Year of Crisis," *International Film Guide 1972*, pp. 63-66, illus.

Rodrigues takes stock of the impact of the Brazilian dictatorship and the crackdown on civil liberties of 1968 in bringing about a virtual end to the original, dynamic, politically and socially committed Cinema Novo movement of the early and mid-sixties. He cites the following causes: censorship, inflation, undeveloped national markets, a disproportionate perecentage of film imports and insufficient exports.

HANS PROPPE AND SUSAN TARR, "Cinema Novo: Pitfalls of Cultural Nationalism," *Jump/Cut* No. 10-11 (June, 1976), pp. 45-48, illus.

A critique of the "internal limitations" of the films of the Northeast—principally Glauber Rocha's *Black God, White Devil* and *Antonio das Mortes*. The authors compare historical background on the figures of the *sertanejo* (backlander), the *santo* or *brato* (mystic), and the *cangaceiro* (bandit) with their film counterparts. They maintain that the Cinema Novo filmmakers err in romanticizing social banditry while overlooking the revolutionary potential of archaic mysticism or "millenarianism" and portraying the peasantry as inert, uninvolved, uncomprehending.

BURNS E. BRADFORD; FRED ESTEVEZ; PETER L. REICH; AND ANNE FLECK, "History in the Brazilian Cinema," *Luso-Brazilian Review* University of Wisconsin Press: Madison) 14.1. Summer, 1977, pp. 49-59.

Three thoughtful essays on themes of dependency, cultural resistance and historical continuity in Brazilian history as seen through four films: *Burn, The Guns, Plantation Boy,* and *Ganga Zumba.*

RANDAL JOHNSON, "Brazilian Cinema Today," *Film Quarterly*, Vol. 31, No. 4, Summer, 1978, pp. 42-45.

A discussion of the "detente" or "rapprochment" between Cinema Novo and post-Cinema Novo filmmakers, on the one hand, and the Brazilian military regime (specifically the state film production and distribution agency, Embrafilme), on the other, and the underlying contradictions of the current situation.

The second part of this brief article examines the two most recent films by leading director Nelson Pereira dos Santos (*The Amulet of Ogum,* 1974, and *Tent of Miracles,* 1977) in order to consider "to what extent filmmakers once associated with Cinema Novo have abandoned their original positions in favor of popular success.

JOHN MOSIER, "The *New* New Brazilian Film," *New Orleans Review*, Volume 6, No. 1 (1978), pp. 3-7.

Using Nelson Pereira dos Santos' work as the basis for a discussion of the current heterogeneity of Brazilian filmmaking, Mosier attempts to convey an insider's view, arguing that "the unity and achievement of Cinema Novo that were celebrated, imitated, and then mourned abroad were illusions based on misunderstandings of what was actually going on in Brazil." Mosier describes the actual situation as the inexpendable, difficult, but increasingly successful quest to capture the national film market and argues that Brazil, alone of all the countries of the Third World, has succeeded in establishing a model of national film development where box office success, international and national prestige, and vertical integration of the industry, are all able to co-exist with one another."

IAN BRUCE, "Cinema censorship," *Index on Censorship*, July-August, 1979, Vol. 8, No. 4, pp. 36-42.

In this excellent article, the problem of film censorship is approached through a broader inquiry into the degree of official control exerted on film production. The author strikes an instructive balance between statistical evidence and the ennumeration of concrete cases, and constructing a broader historical and analytical framework within which the former can be understood.

GLAUBER ROCHA, "Hunger Aesthetics vs. Profit Aesthetics" (translated by Jon Davis), *Framework: A Film Journal*, No. 11, Autumn, 1979, pp. 8-10.

This brief article, originally written in 1967, compares Cinema Novo film production and distribution with the more industrialized situations in Mexico and Argentina.

ROBERT STAM, "Brazilian Avant-Garde Cinema: from *Limite* to *Red Light Bandit*," *Millenium Film Journal*, Summer/Fall, 1979, pp. 33-42, illus.

This article traces the historical antecedents and present-day outlines of the largely *sui generis* avant-garde, experimental and "underground" cinema in Brazil from the 1920s through the 1970s. A detailed description of the acclaimed *Limite* (1930) is followed by a brief discussion of Cinema Novo as an attempt "to synthesize the ideas of the political as well as the cinematic avant-garde" and an analysis of the marked if ambivalent relationship between Cinema Novo and the "underground" film movement. According to Stam, films belonging to this latter category tend to be stylistically pluralistic, generally conflated or parodic, anti-illusionistic, and fascinated with urban mass media and degraded popular culture.

ROBERT STAM AND RANDAL JOHNSON, "Beyond Cinema Novo: Introduction to *Brazil Renaissance* (*Jump/Cut* Special Section)," *Jump/Cut: A Review of Contemporary Cinema*, No. 21, November, 1979, pp. 13-18, illus.

Undoubtedly the most informed and informative essay on Brazilian cinema available in English, this article traces the history of the medium in Brazil from 1896 through the flowering and decline of the Cinema Novo movement (1964-1972) and up to the present day. Reflections on the relevance of the Brazilian situation to the American public frame this history, invoking considerations of the "lack of cultural reciprocity" between the U.S. and Hhird World countries, the "defensive arrogance" of uncomprehending critics, the cultural prescriptiveness of the left, and the debate over what constitutes a genuinely "popular" cinema.

GLAUBER ROCHA, "The History of Cinema Novo" (translated by John Davis), *Framework: A Film Journal*, No. 12, Summer, 1980, (?), pp. 18-27, illus.

In this essay (published October 1969 in *Cine del tercer mundo* under the title "Cinema Novo y la aventura de la creacion") Rocha argues that "every discussion of cinema made outside Hollywood must begin with Hollywood," and proceeds to discuss the cultural conditioning of the Brazilian public and the need for national filmmakers to develop a language which is neither derivative nor populist nor subject to imposed notions of perfection. Written at a critical juncture, when government repression was at its height, this quasi-manifesto also discusses the key role of distribution, the challenge to develop "a hero without a character" the film's relationship to the public, to the critics and to reality: "Cinema Novo has realized that to be *realist* means *discussing the different aspects of the real.*"

DASHA ROSS, "Brazilian Cinema: A Crisis of Direction," *Cinema Papers*, December/January 1979/1980, pp. 609-611, illus.

A polemical and somewhat tendentious assessment of the current situation of film production in Brazil which dismisses Nelson Pereira dos Santos' attempts over the past decade to create films with broader mass appeal as "paternalistic" and a "consolidation of the official policy of patriotic culture." Of the hundreds of films produced in Brazil in the late 1970s, and the dozens of artistic and political integrity, this author grants only one (*Cerebral Destruction*, 1977, no credits given) the distinction of being "the only continuing thread of Cinema Novo."

ROBERT STAM AND ISMAIL XAVIER, "Brazilian Avant Garde: Metacinema in the Triste Tropiques, *Millenium Film Journal*, pp. 82-89, illus.

The second in a series of articles on the Brazilian avant-garde (see Stam, 1979), this essay consists of brief but lucid and suggestive appraisals of six features by four different directors, made between 1969 and 1974. The authors emphasize these films' metacinematic stance and their aggressivity toward the spectator, as conveyed through their militant refusal of the "amenities" of conventional narrative and cinematic practice.

BRAZIL—(Bruno Barreto)

ANDREW HORTON, "Carnival Triumph in Bruno Barreto's *Dona Flor and Her Two Husbands*," *Review*, Nos. 25-26, pp. 122-125.

In placing Bruno Barreto in the company of such luminaries as Aristophanes, Chaucer, Cervantes and Shakespeare, *et. al.*, through the ponderous over-conceptualization of the notion of "carnival triumph," the author ludicrously overburdens this intellectual but insubstantial film.

BRAZIL—(Luis Carlos Barreto)

MARK GINSBURG, "Letter from Rio: A Family Affair," *American Film*, Vol. V, No. 10, September, 1980, pp. 12, 14, 65, illus.

This patronizing essay lurches between a glib attempt to describe the situation of Brazilian filmmaking in general and an outsider's "candid impressions" of leading producer Luis Carlos Barreto ("the biggest cork on the sea of the Brazilian cinema establishment") and his equally cinematic family. Cinema Novo is referred to in passing as "reactionary," socially conscious filmmakers as "a corps of elitist film directors and screenwriters dedicated to packaging social conscience statements that are ultimately more cathartic for filmmaker than viewer," the Brazilian filmgoer as devoted to U.S. films because "they could not be further from reality," and promising young director Bruno Barreto as panting to live in Los Angeles.

BRAZIL—(Alberto Cavalcanti)

GEOFFREY MINISH, "Cavalcanti in Paris," *Sight and Sound*, Vol. 39, No. 3, summer, 1970, pp. 134-35, illus.

A brief review and up-date on the career of Alberto Cavalcanti, an early Brazilian director who made his career in France and England and whose short-lived return to Brazil (1950-1955) helped catalyze the development of the Cinema Novo movement.

BRAZIL—(Joaquim Pedro de Andrade)

J. R. MOLOTNIK, *"Macunaima*: Revenge of the Jungle Freaks," *Jump/ Cut: A Review of Contemporary Cinema*, Nos. 12/13, December 30, 1976, pp. 22-24.

An analysis of Joaquim Pedro de Andrade's *Macunaima* which situates the film in its historical, political and social context within Brazil and exposes the inadequacy of conventional North American readings of the film.

RANDAL JOHNSON, "Macunaíma as Brazilian Hero: Filmic Adaptation as Ideological Radicalization," *Latin American Literary Review*, Vol. VII, No. 13, Fall-Winter, 1978, pp. 38-44.

A comparison of the cultural, historical and ideological contexts which gave rise to Mario de Andrade's novel *Macunaima* (1928), high point of the Brazilian Modernist movement's cultural nationalism, and the film of the same name made four decades later by Joaquim Pedro de Andrade, high point of Cinema Novo's Tropicalist phase. The author examines strategies of filmic adaptation ("the magical, fantastic, animated creatures inhabiting the world [of the novel] have been consistently transformed by the filmmaker into the outcasts of Brazilian society") and their ideological significance.

BRAZIL—(Carlos Diegues)

RANDAL JOHNSON, "Sex, Politics and Culture in *Xica da Silva," Jump/ Cut* Special Section: Brazil Renaissance, Part II, *Jump/Cut: A Review of Contemporary Cinema*, No. 22, May, 1980, pp. 18-20, illus.

An examination of the social, historical and allegorical aspects and ideological contradictions (particularly attitudes toward sexuality, race, and populism) in this extremely successful Brazilian film, motivated by the question: "To what extent [has] this concern with audience appeal stifled or motified the earlier critical vision of Cinema Novo?" Johnson's analysis specifies both the progressive and the regressive elements of Diegues' film.

47

DAN YAKIR, "The Mind of Cinema Novo: Carlos Diegues Interviewed by Dan Yakir," *Film Comment*, Vol. 16, No. 5 (September-October, 1980), pp. 40-44, illus.

Diegues opens this interview with a brief and inexplicably mystifying "history" of Brazilian film in which he categorically (and falsely) maintains that "there was no Brazilian cinema before/the birth of Cinema Novo/" and explains the genesis of that movements as "coincidence." The remainder of the interview focuses briefly on each of the eight feature films of Diegues' 17-year career: *Ganga Zumba, A grande ciudade, Os herdeiros, Joanna francesa, Cuando o carnaval chegar, Xica da Silva, Chuvas de verao* and his latest, *Bye Bye Brazil*. As against film as entertainment or theoretical meditation, Diegues defends a personalist, private cinema and traces his own trajectory from the optimistic quest for freedom of the early Cinema Novo period, through the "sick" pessimism and obsession with death of the more repressive post-1968 period, to his current "recovery" as represented in *Summer Showers* and *Bye Bye Brazil*.

BRAZIL—(Ruy Guerra)

MICHEL CIMENT, "Fuy Guerra," *Second Wave* (New York: Praeger, 1970), pp. 99-109, illus.

Beginning with an allusion to Guerra's African origins (Mozambique) and early training in France, the article moves on to a discussion of his "classical" style and often misundestood innovations in temporal extension and modulation. Although there is a certain analytical acuity to the comments on Guerra's visual style and rhythm, the plot summaries are muddled, the translation choppy, and the poetic aspiration increasingly tiresome as the essay moves through Guerra's filmography, from *Os Cafejestes* (*The Delinquents*) through *Os Fuzis* (*The Guns*) and *Sweet Hunters*.

THOMAS ELSAESSER, "Interview with Ruy Guerra," *Monograph* (London), No. 5, April 1974, pp. 27-33, illus.

A particular intelligent interview which focuses on Guerra's style and technique in his four films (*Os Cafejestes*, 1962; *Os Fuzis*, 1963; *Sweet Hunters*, 1969; *The Gods and the Dead*, 1970). Guerra, one of the masterful cinematographers of the Cinema Novo, also proves to be highly aware and articulate about his art.

"*The Fall*: Formal Innovation and Radical Critique," *Jump/Cut* Special Section: Brazil Renaissance, Part II, *Jump/Cut: A Review of Contemporary Cinema*, No. 22, May, 1979, pp. 20-21, illus.

This analysis of *A Queda* (1978) as a formally innovative and politically audacious work scrutinizes the film's mode of production and its broad range of formal devices with as much eloquence and perceptiveness as it articulates the film's content.

BRAZIL—(Humberto Mauro)

GLAUBER ROCHA, "Humberto Mauro and the Historical Position of Brazilian Cinema," *Framework: A Film Journal*, No. 11, pp. 5-8, illus. (Translated by Jon Davis.)

This translation of an essay originally published in 1963 makes available in English an important example of Glauber Rocha as film critic and historian. A contextualizing critical assessment of the foremost Brazilian film pioneer and his most important feature, *Ganga Bruta* (1933), in Rocha's opinion "one of the twenty best films of all time" and the "single most powerful expression" (read: "inspiration") of the "Cinema Novo" in Brazil.

BRAZIL—(Nelson Pereira dos Santos)

MARSHA KINDER, "*Tent of Miracles*," *Film Quarterly*, Vol. 31, No. 4, Summer, 1978, pp. 45-50, illus.

A detailed and enthusiastic account of this intricate film in which "comprehensive social analysis is combined with a comic tolerance and penetrating humanism reminiscent of Renoir," a film about mythic heroes which "simultaneously demystifies the process of myth-building by showing its corruption," a film which "celebrates crossbreeding and mixed forms as the best solution to racism, democracy, and filmmaking."

SEBASTIAN DOMINGUEZ, "Brazilian Cinema Re-awakens: An Interview with Nelson Pereira Dos Santos," *Film Library Quarterly*, Vol. 12, No. 1, 1979, pp. 29-42, illus.

A terse, matter-of-fact interview in which this prolific Brazilian filmmaker, "dean" of the Cinema Novo movement, describes nuts-and-bolts aspects of filmmaking in contemporary Brazil.

BRAZIL—(Glauber Rocha)

"Cinema Novo vs. Cultural Colonialism: An Interview with Glauber Rocha," *Cineaste*, Vol. IV, No. 1, Summer, 1970, pp. 2-9 and 35, illus.

The bulk of this interview concentrates on the politics of film culture: Hollywood dominance over world film production with Brazil as a specific case in point. Rocha is at his most complacent and also occasionally either obtuse, elusive or genuinely confused, so the interview is suffused by a tension between the parties. Rocha's resistance to systematization of any kind—including intellectual coherence—comes through clearly.

ERNEST CALLENBACH, "Comparative Anatomy of Folk Myth Films: *Robin Hood* and *Antonio das Mortes*," *Film Quarterly*, Vol. XXIII, No. 2, Winter, 1969-70, pp. 42-47, illus.

A thoughtful critique, if a somewhat reductionist one, which uses Michael Curtiz' 1938 version of *The Adventres of Robin Hood* as its point of Anglo-Saxon folk-mythic departure to offer an exegesis of Rocha's *Antonio das Mortes*. Callenbach, wary of the easy acclaim which the film received as "revolutionary," sets up "tentative symbolic equivalences" for the social and psychological roles represented by the characters and argues that the viewpoint of the film is in fact traditional, mystifying, more a product of despair than of genuine political analysis. Considering Rocha's other mature works as well, Callenbach finds his central thematic concern to be "the emotional stasis that precedes revenge upon father figures" and perceives a tension between the realistic photographic style and the "mystical, operatic structure" of Rocha's films.

MICHEL CIMENT, "Glauber Rocha," *Second Wave* (New York: Praeger, 1970), pp. 110-119, illus.

On the basis of Rocha's first four films (*Barravento*; *Black God, White Devil*; *Land in Anguish* and *Antonio das Mortes*). Ciment sees Rocha's central thematic preoccupation as the religious alienation of the Brazilian people. He finds Rocha's work to be Brechtian in its desire to make the spectator into a critical observer, anti-rhetorical in its exaggerated rhetoric, critical of violence in its very obsession with it, and anti-mystical in its concentration on myth. "Starting from reality, Rocha reaches stylization and fantasy." Ciment concludes that Rocha restores the mystical, the hidden, the surreal to "revolutionary" art.

GORDON HITCHENS, "An Interview with Glauber Rocha," *Filmmakers Newsletter*, Vol. 3, No. 2, September, 1970, pp. 20-25.

In this dense and informative interview, Rocha begins with an appraisal of the Cinema Novo movement as having come of age (or become obsolete, depending on one's reading). He speaks of new directors following the financing, production and distribution strategies established by the original group of ten Cinema Novo directors, but underlines the emphasis on auteurism as contrasted to the "academism" of a unified group movement. He offers an early definition of *"tropicalismo"* (a kind of "anthropological attitude" which conveys "all the color and the fantasy and the humor and the rhythm of the South American people") which he feels characterizes the later Cinema Novo production. He also discusses his own filmmaking and writing plans in great detail, describing three projected films right down to details of financing. (None of these has been made to date.) Lastly, he summaries and to some extent evaluates his own film activity, from his earliest shorts of the fifties through the "promitive" African-made film *The Lion Has Seven Heads* and his "surrealist" Spanish-made *Cabecas Cortadas* (*Severed Heads*).

GORDON HITCHENS, "The Way to Make a Future: A Conversation with Glauber Rocha," *Film Quarterly*, Vol. XXIV, No. 1, Fall, 1970, pp. 27-30, illus.

Rocha rebuts Callenbach's appraisal of *Antonio das Martes* as "static. Wagnerian, and philosophically idealist," accusing Callenbach of an academic attempt to apply "Lukacsian and Gramscian" versions of Marxist theory as well as a "false Freudianism" to a "Latin American reality [which] is not theoretical but tragic." Disavowing the impact of theory on "the people," Rocha discusses its impact on intellectuals but carefully avoids considering his own role as intellectual and creative artist. He continues to claim that his films are an accurate reflection of Brazilian reality in that they "are not existential films but sociopolitical films of analysis." Yet, in his view, the roots of revolutionary change do not lie in either understanding, analysis or theory (essentially three ways of identifying the same factor) but in "personal agony" which serves as a "provocation to violence." His films seek to capture the Dionysian religious syncretism (Christianity and African religions) which characterizes Brazilian culture, in the vague belief that this mystical energy "will eventually resist oppression."

GLAUBER ROCHA, "Beginning at Zero: Notes on Cinema and Society," *The Drama Review*, Vol. 14, No. 2, Winter, 1970, pp. 144-149, illus.

One of Rocha's more dense and lucid pieces on the theory and the projected practice of Cinema Novo. The overriding theme of the article is the search for an autonomous, decolonized cultural expression: "technically imperfect, dramatically dissonant, poetically rebellious, politically unsure, violent and sad . . .", "a style capable of analyzing, exploring and describing the limits of demonstrating our truth." An unresolved contradiction runs through the essay (and the Cinema Novo movement as well), as seen in Rocha's admission that "the search for our truth has as its price our audience's lack of understanding." Though more faithful to Brazilian culture, the style of the Cinema Novo is essentially imposed from above by a privileged sector of filmmakers upon a public whose tastes have been formed (i.e., deformed) by cultural exports from the U.S.

"CABECAS CORTADAS: A Propos Political Cinema; A Castle in the Third World" (Interview with Rocha), *Afterimage*, No. 3, Summer, 1971, pp. 68-77, illus.

Rocha discusses political cinema, problems of objectivity and immediate efficacy.

"We are the Harbingers of Revolution: An Interview with Glauber Rocha," *Atlas* (reprinted from *The Manchester Guardian*), October, 1971, pp. 54-55, illus.

Rocha outlines his film activity from *Barravento* to *Cabecas Cortadas* and discusses his difficulties with the Brazilian government and his decision to leave Brazil.

JACK FISHER, "Politics by Magic: ANTONIO DAS MORTES," *The Film Journal*, Vol. 1, Spring, 1971, pp. 32-47, illus.

After expending half of his two-page text on a not-so-tongue-in-cheek attempt to construe *Antonio* as a deviant member of the western genre, followed by some confused notions about *macumba* (Afro-Brazilian folk religion) and some arbitrary "parallels" to the work of European directors, Fisher concludes his piece inveighing against audiences who "refuse to accept a work of art on its own terms." The irony of this self-righteous stance completely escapes him. He concludes that *Antonio* "is a major film," but never even attempts to explain why.

JAMES ROY MACBEAN, "VENT D'EST or Godard and Rocha at the Crossroads," *Sight and Sound*, Vol. 40, No. 3, Summer, 1971, pp. 144-150, illus.

An impressive interpretation of Godard's "theoretical practice" as revealed in his post-May '68 feature *Vent D'est* (*Wind from the East*). The article is framed by a discussion of the "crossroads" sequence in this film, in which Rocha plays a "pivotal" role. The body of the article offers a convincing rebuttal to an interpretive article on the film written by the Brazilian director and concludes with a criticism of the "spontaneous," "messianic" line which Rocha represents among Third World filmmakers. A major strength of the article is its resounding critique of bourgeois cinema's adulation and manipulation of emotional response at the expense of the viewers' critical intelligence, an insight which lies at the root of any attempt to create a revolutionary, non-bourgeois form of film expression.

THOMAS KAVANAUGH, "Imperialism and the Revolutionary Cinema:

Glauber Rocha's ANTONIO DAS MORTES," *Journal of Modern Literature*, Vol. 3, No. 2, April, 1973, pp. 201-213.

A thought provoking contribution to the debate on *Antonio das Mortes* which takes Callenbach's article (*Film Quarterly*, Vol. XXIII, No. 2) as its point of departure. Accusing Callenbach of cultural ethnocentrism, "cannibalism" and, finally, "neo-Stalinism" for his attempt to "neutralize" the film-text by applying external criteria for revolutionary change, Kavanaugh himself falls into the same trap by the end of the article, calling Rocha a "revolutionary" director without ever defining his use of the term (something Callenbach deserves credit for attempting). The entire debate points up the absurdity of trying to discuss revolutionary filmmaking outside its proper context (its process of production and re-integration into the national cultural arena). Kavanaugh does, however, make an important contribution in underlining the relativism and cultural ethnocentrism of any critical response which claims to be "universal."

RENE GARDIES, "Structural Analysis of a Textual System: Presentation of a Method" (translated from *Image et Son* by Diana Matias), *Screen*, Vol. 15, No. 1, Spring, 1974, pp. 11-13.

An early application of the analytical methodology derived from Christian Metz' *Langage et Cinema*, this essay has "as its principle to consider the films of Glauber Rocha as one single plurifilmic text, and as its object, to establish the *system* of that text." The films' political and mythic structure is analyzed through a study of character and narrative based on Levi-Strauss' structural approach to myth. The article also includes an analysis of the dramatic and expressive (formal) structure and the "choreography" of the films. Schematic tables abound. Gardies' article is the most methodologically deliberate and suggestive of those to appear in English on Rocha, though in style and organization it still bears the stamp of a work in progress, thus depriving its reader of the alliance between the "pleasures of the intellect" and the "pleasures of the senses" which the author identifies and attempts to deconstruct in the films of Glauber Rocha. (For further elaboration and application of the principles applied here, see No. 79 of the *Cinema d'Aujourdhui* series by the same author.)

ROBERT STAM, "LAND IN ANGUISH: Revolutionary Lessons," *Jump/ Cut*, Nos. 10-11, June, 1976, pp. 49-51, illus.

An intricate appreciation of Glauber Rocha's *Terra em Transe* which identifies the "central dialectic" of the film as "art on the one hand, and social reality on the other," and the "basic aesthetic strategy" of the film as "anti-realist" and "anti-illusionist."

WILLIAM F. VAN WERT, "Ideology in the Third World Cinema: A

Study of Sembene Ousmane and Glauber Rocha," *Quarterly Review of Film Studies*, Vol. 4, No. 2, Spring, 1979, pp. 207-226.

This suggestive examination of the relationship between cinema and ideology in two leading filmmakers from the Third World begins with a consideration of the theoretical and artistic successes and failures of Eisenstein. Van Wert contrasts the Soviet director's use of "fixed typage" to Rocha's and Sembene's "structural typage" and contends that this difference accounts for the "closed" ideology of the Eisenstein films and for the more "open" ideology of films made by the Brazilian and the Senegalese. "Where Eisenstein creates an artificial synthesis to a basically Hegelian dialectic through a director-imposed montage instead of through a denotative synthesis within the film (...), Rocha and Sembene replace the terminal synthesis of Eisenstein with the beginning of another dialectic." Concentrates on Rocha's first feature, *Barravento* (1961) and on Sembene's *Emitai* (1970).

GRAHAM BRUCE, "Music in Glauber Rocha's Films," *Brazilian Renaissance*, Part 2 (*Jump/Cut* Special Section), *Jump/Cut: A Review of Contemporary Cinema*, No. 22, May, 1980, pp. 15-18, illus.

A richly detailed examination of Rocha's use of music as a "vital element," "a means of both structuring sequences and of commenting on the images which comprise those sequences," rather than a mere corroboration of the image. Impressive musical erudition is combined with a solid grasp of Brazilian culture and the visual components of film. Concentrates on the director's foremost features: *Barravento* (1961), *Black God, White Devil* (1963), *Land in Anguish* (1967), and *Antonio das Mortes* (1969).

BRAZIL—(Orlando Senna)

DON RANVAUD, "Interview With Orlando Senna," *Framework: A Film Journal*, No. 12, pp. 31-32.

A rather disjointed interview with the Brazilian filmmaker (who collaborated with Jorge Bodansky on the excellent *Iracema*) which concentrates on his latest film *Diamante Bruta*, though mysteriously withholding the title until halfway through the exchange.

CHILE—(General)

AUGUSTO MARTINEZ TORRES AND MANUEL PEREZ ESTREMERA, "Chile: Introduction to Chilean Cinema," *CTVD* (*Cinema-TV Digest*), No. 33, Fall, 1972, pp. 31-32.

A brief introduction to film in Chile up to the first year of the Popular Unity government by the authors of *Nuevo cine latinoamericano.*

JULIANNE BURTON, "The Promised Land Denied: Towards a History of the New Chilean Cinema From Its Origins to 1973," January, 1974, 14 pp.

A summary of Chilean filmmaking with an emphasis on the period up to and during Allende's Popular Unity government. The second part of the article discusses the work of the two major directors under Allende, Miguel Littin and Raul Ruiz, in some detail.

DON RANVAUD, "Introduction to Latin America I: Chile," *Framework: A Film Journal,* No. 10, Spring, 1979, pp. 11-12.

An intelligent and, in its short scope, highly suggestive account (if slightly encumbered by an overblown "cinema-ese" *a la Screen*) of the theoretical implications of the political-filmic practice of three leading Chilean directors: Helvio Soto, Miguel Littin, and Patricio Guzman.

PETER SCHUMANN, "Chilean Cinema in Exile," *Framework: A Film Journal,* No. 10, Spring, 1979, p.p. 13-14. (Translated by Robin Mann.)

A brief summary of feature and documentary production by exiled Chilean filmmakers which designates four main themes in what the author views as the unprecedented case of a national cinema "forced to try to continue its life internationally": emmigration, fascism in Chile, solidarity, reckoning with history and current developments.

MALCOLM COAD, "Rebirth of Chilean Cinema," *Index on Censorship,* Vol. 9, No. 2, April, 1980, pp. 3-8, illus.

A dense and highly informative account of official Chilean policy toward film education, production, distribution and exhibition since the military took over in September, 1973, including summaries of all films made in Chile since that time and the most important works of the Chilean "cinema of resistance" which has grown out of the diaspora of Chilean filmmakers throughout Europe and the Americas.

ZUZANA M. PICK, "Chile: The Cinema of Resistance, 1973-1979," part of a Special Section on Chilean Cinema, *Cine-tracts,* No. 9 (Vol. 3, No. 1), pp. 18-28.

Beginning with a brief survey of works about post-coup Chile produced outside of Chile by non-Chileans, the author proceeds to a discussion of the filmmaking activity of Chileans in exile, part of a movement which they prefer to designate as a "cinema of resistance." A three-page filmography covers the period from 1973-1979. Finally, the author describes and evaluates, in short scope, the work of four leading Chilean filmmakers: Patricio Guzman, Miguel Littin, Helvio Soto, and Raul Ruiz.

ZUZANA M. PICK, "Letter from Guzman to Chris Marker," "Reflections Previous to the Filming of *The Battle of Chile*," "*The Battle of Chile:* A Schematic Shooting Script," Part of a Special Section on Chilean Cinema, *Cine-tracts*, No. 9 (Vol. 3, No. 1), pp. 35-49.

The most valuable segment of this four-part dossier on Chilean cinema, consisting of original documents from the *Grupo Tercer Año* which originally appeared in *Cine cubano:* the original letter describing the initial project and requesting support, the "manifesto" describing the group's assessment of various documentary methodologies, work rules, a list of original equipment at the group's disposal, and, finally, the original script outline.

CHILE—(Patricio Guzman)

JULIANNE BURTON, "Politics and the Documentary in People's Chile. An Interview with Patricio Guzman on *The Battle of Chile, Specialist Review*, No. 35 (September/October, 1977), pp. 36-68, illus. Reprinted in pamphlet form by the New England Free Press, Sommerville, Mass.).

A thorough discussion of the genesis of this extraordinary three-party documentary in the context of the ideological struggle taking place in the Chilean media and in all sectors of the society during the last year of the Allende regime, with detailed discussion of the methodology, style and content of the film.

UDAYAN GUPTA and *FLQ* Staff, "An Interview with Patricio Guzman, director of "The Battle of Chile,'" *Film Library Quarterly*, Vol. 11, No. 4, 1978, pp. 16-20, illus.

Covers the director's background and the genesis, production process, national and international reception of his three documentaries: *The First Year, The Answer to October*, and parts I and II of *The Battle of Chile*.

PATRICIO GUZMAN, "*La Batalla de Chile: El Golpe*" (translated by Don Ranvaud), *Framework: A Film Journal*, No. 10, Spring, 1979, pp. 3-4, illus.

A very brief account of the strategy, methodology and preparation of *The Battle of Chile*.

PATRICIO GUZMAN, "*The Battle of Chile* III," *Framework: A Film Journal*, No. 11, Summer, 1979, pp. 3-4.

Guzman discusses the "overt and covert scenarios" of the third and final part of his epic documentary, *The Battle of Chile* (*Popular Power*) which describes the variety of alternative institutions created by the workers in respoinse to concrete problems left unsolved by official channels, "a kind of *de facto* socialist 'state' . . . rising about the liberal bourgeois state apparatus and displacing it."

ZUZANA M. PICK, "Interview with Patricio Guzman: *La Batalla de Chile*," part of a Special Section on Chilean Cinema, *Cine-tracts* No. 9 (Vol. 3, No. 1), pp. 29-34.

Covers the conception, planning, filming and editing of Parts I and II of *The Battle of Chile: The Insurrection of the Bourgeoisie* and *The Coup d'Etat*.

CHILE—(Miguel Littin)

"Film in Chile: An Interview with Miguel Littin," *Cineaste*, Vol. IV, No. 4, Spring, 1971, pp. 4-9, illus.

In this interview, which took place in New York only a few months after Allende's Popular Unity government took power, Littin takes a sober view of the forthcoming intensification of class struggle in Chile. He discusses the genesis of his first feature, *The Jackal of Nahueltoro* (1968) and its impact, and briefly describes plans for a film which eventually became *The Promised Land* (1973).

JULIANNE BURTON, "THE PROMISED LAND," *Film Quarterly*, Vol. XXIX, No. 1, Fall, 1975, pp. 57-61, illus.

A comprehensive review of Chile's only film epic (and the process of making it) which emphasizes the film's adulation/critique of popular culture and its exploration of the most pressing problems facing Chile under Allende through historical parallels with the situation in the thirties, the era in which Littin situates his film.

ROBERT SCOTT, "The Arrival of the Instrument in Flesh and Blood: Deconstruction in Littin's *The Promised Land*," *Cine-tracts*, Vol. 1, No. 4, Spring-Summer, 1978, pp. 81-97, illus.

The first part of this two-part essay consists of an at times abstruse and belabored meditation on "the ways in which ideology is made invisible and pervasive through cinematic forms" and the necessity for formulating "those theories which will allow, even facilitate, the emergence of a genuinely Marxist cinema." The second and most valuable part, on techniques of deconstruction in *The Promised Land*, though somewhat handicapped by the author's unfamiliarity with

Chilean history and culture, offers a useful short-by-shot reading of several key sequences in this important film, "a text in crisis, ... in which parallel lines of emotional and intellectual structure continually interact and comment upon one another." Scott concludes that "as a model for a cinema which attempts both to reach the masses and to provide them with a simultaneous critique of that reaching [*The Promised Land*] is unsurpassed."

KATHERINE S. KOVACS, "Miguel Littin's *Recurso del metodo:* The Aftermath of Allende," *Film Quarterly*, Vol. XXX, No. 3, Spring, 1980, pp. 22-29, illus.

A brief account of this leading Chilean director's first three feature films—*The Jackal of Nahueltoro* (1969), *The Promised Land* (1973), and *Letters from Marusia* (1976)—precedes a more lengthy discussion of *Reasons of State* (also called *Viva el Presidente* in English, 1978) a Cuban-Mexican-French co-production based on the novel by Cuba's foremost novelist, Alejo Carpentier. The author concludes that this "Brechtian" film, both "lavish" and "mechanical," is "ultimately a Latin American morality play, in which the forces of left and right respond in predetermined patterns." Though conceived as a meditation on "such fundamental elements of the Latin American experience as dependency, dictatorship, and imperialism," she argues that the film changes its tone at the end to offer instead a wistful glimpse of the condition of exile, debilitating and degrading even for a "despicable tyrant" because "in exile both dictators and revolutionaries are out of the fray, bypassed by history ..."

CHILE—(Raul Ruiz)

RICHARD ROUD, "Turning Points: Ruiz and Truffaut," *Sight and Sound*, Vol. 47, No. 3, Summer, 1978, pp. 163-166, illus.

Enthusiastic appraisals of *La Vocation Supreme* and *The Hypothesis of the Stolen Painting*, French-made feature films by one of the most important exiled Chilean feature directors.

DON RANVAUD, "Interview with Paul Ruiz," *Framework: A Film Journal*, No. 10, spring, 1979, pp. 16-18, 27, illus. (Translated by Cristina Weller.)

An engaging and valuable interview with this most productive and yet least easily viewed of Chilean feature filmmakers, now working in the French film industry but still virtually unknown in North America.

CHILE—(Antonio Skarmeta)

JOHN MOSIER, "Art, Film, and Reality: An Interview With Antonio Skarmeta," *New Orleans Review,* Vol. 7, No. 3, Fall, 1980, pp. 257-260.

Fiction and screenwriter Antonio Skarmeta discusses the political situation in Chile under Allende, particularly as it applied to the national film production company, Chile Films. Skarmeta details what he sees as the three-stage evolution of this agency, discusses the production of Patricio Guzman's *The Battle of Chile* and his own collaboration with German director Peter Lilienthal on *La victoria* and *Calm Prevails Over the Country,* and concludes with his future plans for film and fiction writing. Apparently a direct transcription, without benefit of editing, the syntax is unmistakably and unnecessarily Spanish throughout.

CUBA—(General)

PETER BROOK, "The Cuban Enterprise," *Sight and Sound,* Vol. 30, No. 2, Spring, 1961, pp. 78-79, illus.

In these first-hand impressions of the nascent Cuban film industry, this director discusses the first two features (Tomas Gutierrez Alea's *Stories of the Revolution* and Julio Garcia Espinosa's *Cuba Dances*), as well as related film activity, capturing the enthusiasm and excitement, but missing some of the political motivation. His attempt to set "the Cuban enterprise" into the context of the non-existent Latin American film market ("not even the beginnings of a serious Latin film audience") completely ignores questions of neo-colonial cultural conditioning and thus obscures more than it clarifies.

ELIZABETH SUTHERLAND, "Cinema of Revolution—90 Miles from Home," *Film Quarterly,* Vol. XVI, No. 2, Winter, 1961-62, pp. 42-49, illus.

This survey of the first three years of post-revolutionary Cuban filmmaking is now past history, but the scope of the article and the author's perceptivity make it far from obsolete. In addition to an overview and critical appraisal of early documentary and feature production, summaries culled from *Cine cubano* of the theoretical positions of three major cineastes (Alfredo Guevara, Julio Garcia Espinosa and Tomas Gutierrez Alea), and a survey of the foreign films then on view in Havana, the article now offers the additional sport of measuring Sutherland's predictions and projected reservations against the subsequent accomplishments of Cuban cinematography.

WILLIAM JOHNSON, "Report from Cuba," *Film Quarterly*, Vol. XIX, No. 4, Summer, 1966, pp. 31-36.

A disconnected, snide and uncomprehending account which obscures more than it illuminates.

MARIA EULALIA DOUGLAS, "The Cuban Cinema," *Take One*, Vol. I, No. 12, July-August, 1968, pp. 6-9, illus.

A broad—if necessarily somewhat superficial—account of post-revolutionary film production, with appropriate emphasis on related activities in film exhibition and education. Includes brief bio-filmographies of four major directors: Julio Garcia Espinosa, Tomas Gutierrez Alea, Santiago Alvarez and Humberto Solas.

ANDI ENGEL, "Solidarity and Violence," *Sight and Sound*, Vol. 38, No. 4, Autumn, 1969, pp. 197-200, illus.

Written on the occasion of a week-long Cuban film festival at London's National Film Theatre (the same festival which was abortively scheduled for New York in the spring of 1972), the article focuses on three Cuban filmmakers: Tomas Gutierrez Alea (*Memories of Underdevelopment*), Humberto Solas (*Lucia*) and documentarist Santiago Alvarez. Writing in a modest conversational style, Engel provides interesting if not extensive information on these three directors, but ends with a kind of limp despair bemoaning the fact that "revolutionary" films are more a product than an agent of revolutionary change.

RENATA ADLER, "Three Cuban Cultural Reports with Films Somewhere in Them" (written in February, 1969), *A Year in the Dark* Berkeley: Medallion Editions, 1971), pp. 364-381.

Valuable more for general orientation than for specifics, these three articles—though they treat the films mentioned in a cursory and often unperceptive manner—contain valuable observations on the general cultural scene at the crucial juncture of 1969, especially regarding the role of the Cuban Film Institute (ICAIC) in that struggle. Fragments of interviews with novelist Elmundo Desnoes (*Memories of Underdevelopment*) and director Humberto Solas (*Lucia*) provide some provocative insights.

JULIO MATAS, "Theater and Cinematography" in Carmelo Mesa-Lago, ed., *Revolutionary Change in Cuba* (Pittsburgh: University of Pittsburgh Press, 1971), pp. 436-442.

A routine and at times naively biased account whose major distinguishing feature is the brief history of filmmaking in *pre-revolutionary* Cuba.

MIKKO PYHALA, "Cuba," *International Film Guide 1971* (London: Tantivy Press), pp. 97-99, illus.

A fine nutshell account of post-revolutionary Cuban film production through 1969 which appends an equally brief but meaty review of Manuel Octavio Gomez' *First Charge of the Machete* (1969) and a brief listing of "forthcoming" films, many of which have never come forth.

GARY CROWDUS, "The Spring 1972 Cuban Film Festival Bust," *Film Society Review*, Vol. 7, Nos. 7-9, March/April/May, 1972, pp. 23-26, illus.

Beginning with a summary of relations between he U.S. and Cuba since Batista's overthrow on New Year's Eve of 1959, the article details events and negotiations up to and including the Treasury Department's film seizure on the second day which brought the festival to an abrupt halt. Crowdus' concluding optimism for a speedy decision on American Documentary Films' (sponsor of the festival) suit against the Treasury Department and the prompt rescheduling of the festival was never justified in fact.

PIERRE SAUVAGE, "Cine cubano," *Film Comment*, spring, 1972, pp. 24-31, illus. (See also, "Letter to the Editor," *Film Comment*, September/October, 1972, pp. 75-76.)

Sauvage "intercuts" information on the Cuban film industry with brief appraisals of Cuban films viewed at the Cinematheque Francaise (the same "package" shown in London and foiled in New York) and observations by filmmakers who chose to work outside Cuba. Sardonic at times without ceasing to be informative. The "Leter to the Editor" contains important recifications.

JORGE AYALA BLANCO, "Cine Cubano: Revaluaciones, Devaluaciones y Presentaciones" (translated from *Siempre!* by Ken Eisler), *Movietone News* (Seattle Film Society), No. 37, November, 1974, pp. 14-15.

A succinct reappraisal by a major Mexican film critic of seven Cuban features (*Days of Water, The Adventures of Juan Quin Quin, Man from Maisinicu, The New School, Bay of Pigs,* and briefly, *Memories of Underdevelopment* and *Lucia*) which is of special interest because the first film discussed is still not available in the U.S.

ANDRES HERNANDEZ, "Filmmaking and Politics: The Cuban Experience," *American Behavioral Scientist*, Vol. 17, No. 3, January-February, 1974, pp. 360-392. (Also available from *Cineaste*; 17 pp.).

This excellent article provides the groundwork for a systematic analysis of the role played by cinema in the process of political socialization in post-revolutionary Cuba. The author best describes the piece: "The paper focuses primarily on documenting the changes brought by the Revolution in terms of the institutional setting for filmmaking and distribution, output, training of technicians and directors, use of film in educational activities, form and content of locally produced features and documentaries ... with particular emphasis on the use of cinema as a political instrument and the relationship of Cuban films to the cultural revolution." Succinct and well-documented, the article includes tables, bibliography and an appendix on ICAIC feature film production from 1960-1973.

LOURDES CASAL AND MARVIN SURKIN, "Recent Cuban Cinema," *Cineaste*, Vol. VI, No. 4, Spring, 1975, pp. 22 and 51, illus.

A first-hand report on the most important Cuban film production of 1974 which concentrates on two full-length documentaries (*Viva la Republica* and *The New School*) and two features (*Man from Maisinicu* and *Ustedes Tienen la Palabra*).

ANDRES R. HERNANDEZ, "The Role of Film in Cuban Development," in Jean Marie Ackerman, ed., *Films of a Changing World: A Critical International Guide*, Vol. 11, Washington, D C.: Society for International Development, pp. 24, 25.

Written in the early 1970s, this article identifies Cuban cinema as "simultaneously a means toward development, a witness to the development process, and an instrument for analyzing the process." In very brief scope, the article discusses pre-revolutionary antecedents, short and full-length documentary production, mobile cinema, two feature films (*Memories of Underdevelopment* and *Lucia*) and provides a description of five films which deal with developmental themes.

JULIANNE BURTON, "Twenty Years of Revolutionary Cuban Cinema: An Introduction," *Jump/Cut* Special Section on Twenty Years of Revolutionary Cuban Cinema, Part I, *Jump/Cut: A Review of Contemporar Cinema*, No. 19, December, 1978, pp. 17-20, illus.

An overview of the history, ideology and formal practice of filmmaking in Cuba which begins a brief look at the pre-revolutionary situation before dividing the post-revolutionary period into four phases and attempting to characterize each in some detail.

JOHN MRAZ, "*Lucia*: Visual Style and Historical Portrayal" *Jump/Cut* Special Section on Twenty Years of Revolutionary Cuban Cinema, Part I, *Jump/Cut: A Review of Contemporary Cinema*, No. 19, December, 1978, pp. 21-27, illus.

An attempt to break with "literary models" of filmic analysis, this ground-breaking article reproduces and serially comments upon 59 frame enlargements from this now classic film. This unusual example of politically-informed formalist analysis (its categories range from "Segment Opening Shots" and "High Angle Shots" to "Human Relations: Women; Women and Men; Race") bases itself on the contention that "the use of multiple styles [characteristic of Cuban filmmaking of this period] has crucial epistemological implications—the most important of which are an insistence upon dialectical thinking and the recognition that consciousness realized itself at the level of perception."

MICHAEL CHANAN, "Cuban Images: An Introduction," *Framework: A Film Journal*, No. 10, Spring, 1979, pp. 19-22.

This introduction is interesting not so much for the range of concrete information provided but—as is characteristic of Chanan's work—for the thoughtfulness, sincerity and insight of its "digressions." His account of Cuban cinema as "one of the most powerful means of social cohesion" offers some basic statistics, describes the genesis and organizational structure of the Cuban Film Institute (ICAIC), and offers a tentative thematic typology of Cuban feature films. Most unique and thought-provoking, however, is the section which assesses Fidel's presence in Cuban films, concluding that his relationship with the Cuban people "constitutes the confluence of politics and entertainment." Chanan's inability to study Cuban cinema without simultaneously interrogating all aspects of Cuban society, politics and personality is to be admired.

ZUZANA M. PICK, "Towards a Renewal of Cuban Revolutionary Cinema: A Discussion of Cuban Cinema Today," *Cine-tracts*, Nos. 7-8, pp. 21-31 (Vol. 2, Nos. 3-4), Fall 1979.

In this discussion, conducted in Canada in early 1978, two of the most influential Cuban cineastes—Tomas Gutierrez Alea and Jorge Fraga, the latter Director of Production at the Cuban Film Institute—address topics which range from the influence of Cuban cinema on filmmaking in other Latin American countries and the Third World, to the integration of documentary and fictional modalities, to notions of history in cinema. The filmmakers offer candid assessments of the accomplishments and limitations of the revolutionary Cuban film project, and conclude with some provocative reflections on the relevance of theoretical research in structuralism and semiotics as currently evolving in the non-socialist world to the interests and aims of Cuban filmmaking.

PHILLIP TERZIAN, "Cuba in Panavision," *Harper's*, Vol. 258, No. 1544, January, 1979, pp. 28-30.

Sardonic reminiscences of an unrepentant cynic, member of the first delegation of U.S. film critics to visit Cuba in June of 1978.

JORGE SILVA, "Film Criticism in Cuba: An Interview with Enrique Colina, *Jump/Cut* Special Section on Twenty Years of Revolutionary Cuban Cinema, Part III, *Jump/Cut: A Review of Contemporary Cuban Cinema*, No. 22, May, 1980, pp. 32-33. (Translated by Julianne Burton.)

Enrique Colina hosts a popular prime-time television show called "Twenty-four Times a Second" which deals critically with films of current interest. In this interview with a Colombian documentarist, Colina discusses the premises of the program: "We try to perform a kind of aesthetic and ideological 'de-montage,' taking apart what the filmmaker has assembled in order to reveal the film's inner workings."

TOM WAUGH, "Joris Ivens' Work in Cuba: *Travel Notebook* and *A People in Arms*," *Jump/Cut* Special Section on Twenty Years of Revolutionary Cuban Cinema, Part III, *Jump/Cut: A Review of Contemporary Cinema*, No. 22, May, 1980, pp. 25-29, illus.

A rare and telling glimpse into filmmaking in Cuba in the second year of the revolution, through the experience of a politically-committed documentarist of international range and renown. A full and lively description of Ivens' two Cuban films is followed by reminiscenes of some of the now-prominent Cuban filmmakers who then made up Ivens' inexperienced crew.

CUBA—(Santiago Alvarez)

"Five Frames Are Five Frames, Not Six, But Five: An Interview with Santiago Alvarez," *Cineaste*, Vol. No. 4, Spring, 1975, pp. 16-21, illus.

Santiago Alvarez, world-famous documentarist and head of Cuba's weekly Latin American Newsreel since its inception in 1959, discusses his own recent work (*De America soy hijo y a ella me debo* and *Y el Cielo Fue Tomado por Asalto*), aspects of ICAIC, and his belief in the imminent obsolescence of the film medium as we know it.

STUART HOOD, "Murder on the Way; Santiago Alvarez Season at NFT," *New Statesman*, April 18, 1980, p. 596, illus.

A dense and penetrating assessment of the work of this Cuban documentarist on the occasion of the major Alvarez retrospective at the British National Film Theater in the spring of 1980.

EMILIO L. MENDEZ AND MIGUEL ORODEA, "Cinema and Revolution: Talking with Santiago Alvarez," *Issues: A Monthly Review of International Affairs*, May, 1980, pp. 18-21, illus.

A somewhat disjointed interview conducted in London in April of 1980, made even more so by the interview's own curious, choppy style of "montage." The role of sound in cinematic language, improvisation, emotional versus rational filmic elements, the importance of the newsreel format for young revolutionary societies, and the parallels between the Cuban and the Nicaraguan revolutions are the major topics addressed here.

CUBA—(Julio Garcia Espinosa)

JULIO GARCIA ESPINOSA, "For an Imperfect Cinema," *Afterimage*, No. 3, Summer, 1971, pp. 54-67, illus.

This essay is one of the two major theoretical documents to emerge from the militant cinema movement in Latin America to date. (The other in Solanas' and Getino's "Toward a Third Cinema.") Written in 1969 as a complement to the practical experience of filming *The Adventures of Juan Quin Quin,* Garcia Espinosa's essay examines the nature and practice of art in contemporary society, and specifically how the development of science, the social pressur of the masses, and the revolutionary potential of the contemporary world combine to "abolish forever the concept and the reality of the 'elite' in art." He distinguishes between mass and popular art and discusses the prospects for art as the province of all human beings. The author calls for the demise of the *auteur* and the critic and the substitution of an audience-creator in struggle and a cinema of *process* rather than *a priori* analysis.

JULIO GARCIA ESPINOSA, "For an Imperfect Cinema" (translated by Julianne BURTON), *Jump/Cut* Special Section on Twenty Years of Revolutionary Cuban Cinema, Part II, *Jump/Cut: A Review of Contemporary Cinema,* No. 20, May, 1979, pp. 24-26, illus. (see 1971 for earlier appearance in Einglish).

This re-translation of one of the two most important theoretical pieces to come out of the New Latin American Cinema movement (the other is Fernando Solanas' and Octavio Getino's "Towards a Third Cinema") includes sections deleted from the earlier *Afterimage* version.

ANNA MARIE TAYLOR, "Imperfect Cinema, Brecht, and *The Adventures of Juan Quin Quin,*" *Jump/Cut* Special Section on Twenty Years of Revolutionary Cuban Cinema, Part II, *Jump/Cut: A Review of Contemporary Cinema,* No. 20, May, 1979, pp. 26-29, illus.

An interpretation of Julio Garcia Espinosa's theory of "imperfect cinema" through an analysis of the film which prompted the writing of that thoretical essay. Taylor analyzes *The Adventures of Juan Quin*

Quin as an episodic, parodic series of picaresque escapades through different cinematic genres. She criticizes the film and the theory: "The relationship between spectacle and audience as participants and creators remains problematic"; "A satiric political film about culture paradoxically makes evident how much generic structures maintain themselves intact and resist deconstruction"; "*Juan Quin Quin* also fails to keep satire from annexing what were apparently meant to be politically serious sequences." The essay concludes with a comparison between the "aesthetic politics" of Garcia Espinosa and Bertolt Brecht.

CUBA—(Sergio Giral)

JULIANNE BURTON AND GARY CROWDUS, "Cuban Cinema and the Afro-Cuban Heritage: An Interview with Sergio Giral," *The Black Scholar*, Vol. 8, Nos. 8-10, Summer, 1977, pp. 62-72, illus.

In this interview, Cuba's leading black filmmaker discusses the years he spent in New York City, the inception of his filmmaking career, his documentary training, and the genesis of his important first feature, *The Other Francisco* (1974).

FRANCINE MASIELLO, "*The Other Francisco*: Film Lessons on Novel Reading," *Ideologies and Literature*, Vol. 1, No. 5, January/February, 1978, pp. 19-27.

A limited mastery of cinematic vocabulary and certain fundamental inaccuracies regarding the plot of this particular film are relatively minor limitations which are offset by the sharp critical intelligence of this deeply suggestive piece which analyzes *The Other Francisco* as "an exercise in seeing and reading which tests the limits of narrative reliability." According to the author, "Segments of *The Other Francisco* critically decode the bourgeois novel which inspired it while diverse cinematic sequences comment on and correct one another. The film's self-conscious exegetic experiments and its recuperation of historical realities produce a highly sophisticated drama, unique in cinematic form."

CUBA—(Manuel Octavio Gomez)

JULIANNE BURTON, "Popular Culture and Perpetual Quest: An Interxiew with Manuel Octavio Gomez," *Jump/Cut* Special Section of Twenty Years of Revolutionary Cuban Cinema, Part II, *Jump/Cut: A Review of Contemporary Cinema*, No. 20, May, 1979, pp. 17-20, illus.

Though not as well known outside Cuba as his colleagues Tomas Gutierrez Alea and Humberto Solas, Gomez ranks with them as one of the three leading Cuban feature directors. In this interview, he describes his life-long interest in sociology and popular culture, and his initiation into filmmaking, discussing all his feature films and several documentaries.

JOHN HESS, "The Personal is Political in Cuba: *Now It's Up to You* and *A Woman, A Man, A City*, *Jump/Cut* Special Section on Twenty Years of Revolutionary Cuban Cinema, Part II, *Jump/Cut: A Review of Contemporary Cinema*, No. 20, pp. 15-17, illus.

This analysis of two important Cuban features dealing with issues of contemporary life begins with brief plot summaries, then proceeds to a consideration of Gomez' use of traditional narrative forms while simultaneously transforming them by reversing conventional "narrative flok." Hess concludes with a critique of Gomez' idealized use of women as symbols and icons to the exclusion of more fallible (and hence realistic) characterizations.

CUBA—(Sarah Gomez)

JULIA LESAGE, "*One Way or Another:* Dialectical, Revolutionary, Feminist," *Jump/Cut* Special Section on Twenty Years of Revolutionary Cuban Cinema, Part II, *Jump/Cut: A Review of Contemporary Cinema*, No. 20, May, 1979, pp. 20-23, illus.

After an opening meditation on the meaning of the Marxist concept *dialectics*, Lesage goes on to illustrate how the concept functions in terms of plot, characterization, narrative and cinematic structure in what is to date the only Cuban feature film made by a woman.

CUBA—(Tomas Gutierrez Alea)

JAY COCKS AND DAVID DENBY, eds., "The Alea Affair," *Film 73/74: An Anthology of the National Society of Film Critics* (Indianapolis: Bobbs Merrill, 1974), pp. xiv-xvii.

A brief introduction and three documents on the National Society of Film Critics' attempt to present a special prize and cash award to Tomas Gutierrez Alea for *Memories of Underdevelopment*: David Binder, *New York Times*, "U.S. Refuses Visa to Cuban Director to Get Film Award," telegram from Tomas Gutierrez Alea explaining his absence at the ceremonies, and the presidential speech by Andrew Sarris at the awards ceremonies.

"Three on Two: Henry Fernandez, David I. Grossvogel and Emir Rodriguez Monegal on Desnoes and Alea," *Diacritics: A Review of Contemporary Criticism*, Vol. 4, No. 4, Winter, 1074, pp. 51-55, 55-60 and 60-64.

The first of these three essays, by Emir Rodriguez Monegal, concentrates on the author's chosen realm of comparative literary criticism, thus providing some insight into the original novel but very little into the subsequent film. Characterizing the film's style as a "Marxist neorealism" derived from the Italians, and criticizing it for excluding "the dimension of the fantasy" (often present, in fact, throughout the film) Rodriguez Monegal concludes that the international acclaim which has been conferred on both the novel and the film is a result of a "poetic misunderstanding," and takes the opportunity to conclude with a list of his own literary favorites, accompanied by the unsupported contention that they constitute "truly revolutionary art."

The second essay, by Henry Fernandez, treats the film in much greater detail and shows greater sensitivity to its meaning and modalities, though, again, the approach is somewhat over-literary. As a narrative exegesis which fails to take the formal elements of the film into careful account, portions of this interpretation are, to say the least, debatable.

David Grossvogel again devotes his major energies to an analysis of the novel, offering many valid criticisms independent of his insistence on grounding his remarks in Lukacs' and Trotsky's theories of literature and in arbitrary "parallels" between Desnoes and Andre Gide. Grossvogel acknowledges that the best analysis of the film is the director's own "Working Notes." Though he quotes from them at length, he might have done better to reprint them wholesale, for his own view of the film never emancipates itself from the misleading and falsely construed "archetype" of the novel .

JULIA LESAGE, "Images of Underdevelopment," *Jump/Cut*, No. 1, May-June, 1974, pp. 9-11, illus.

A lengthy appraisal of *Memories of Underdevelopment* which focuses on the themes of underdevelopment and sexual politics. Generally accurate in its interpretation, though not without certain crucial errors (Elena is *not* pregnant when her family brings Sergio to court; the Russian tourists *are* present at the Hemingway museum; the Bay of Pigs documentary sequence is *not* "seemingly unrelated to the narrative" since Sergio is in fact the narrator). The final paragraph raises the crucial question of how reception and interpretation of the film differ according to the cultural context in which the film is viewed.

JULIANNE BURTON, "MEMORIES OF UNDERDEVELOPMENT: Alienation and Critical Response, Of Can a Bourgeois Intellectual Find Happiness in a Revolutionary Society?", *Review* (Center for Inter-American Relations), Fall, 1976, pp. 51-61.

Beginning with a critical look at U.S. critical response to the film, this article moves on to an account of the film's genesis (both literary and extraliterary) and, finally, aims at a comprehensive interpretation of the film itself.

MARGOT KERNAN, "Cuban Cinema: Tomas Guiterrez Alea" [sic], *Film Quarterly*, Vol. XXIX, No. 2, Winter, 1976, pp. 45-52, illus.

Taking her cue from an Eisenstein text, Kernan sets out to examine how three feature films by Tomas *Gutierrez* Alea (she misspells his name throughout) "present a specifically Latin American view of 'phenomena of class-reflected reality" and "to understand how these films function as a discourse which oscillates between a public and private view of events, between the overtly political and the apolitical position." *Memories of Underdevelopment*, a film "with a logic we must discover for ourselves," gets the lengthiest treatment, but the internal logic of this complex film remains unelucidated because Kernan loses herself in occasionally contradictory detail. (How can she assert, for instance, that Sergio is a "political partisan" and yet agree with Desnoes that he never becomes involved in reality?)

The second section on *Death of a Bureaucrat*, is also plagued by impression. A large chunk of the film's daring is lost when Kernan identifies as busts of Lenin what are in fact statues of Cuba's foremost revolutionary hero and poet, Jose Marti, leader of the independence struggle against the Spaniards.

What is most admirable about the article—its attempt to relate the content of these films to he larger realities of Cuban hisory, economy and revolutionary necessity—is handicapped by a superficial knowledge of all three.

THOMAS M. KAVANAGH, "Dialectics and the Textuality of Class Conflict," *Journal of Latin American Lore*, Vol. 4, No. 1, 1978, pp. 135-143.

An extremely intelligent and perceptive analysis of this much-scrutinized film as "the story of an elite in dissolution," "an analysis of the elaboration and obfuscation of individuality in relation to a surrounding group," and "a study of media within a revolutionary society." Kavanagh demonstrates many insights into the character and role of the alienated bourgeois protagonist, Sergio, whose "specific tragedy is the attempt at an impossible synthesis."

What initially appears to be a relatively mechanical obeissance to the journal's editor's concept of cinema as a form of "elite lore" ("non-institutionalized knowledge") becomes in fact a powerful refutation when Kavanagh concludes that, "As a film, *Memories of Underdevelopment* shows us that the distinction between folk and elite is a myth. . . . To attempt to study eliterole and folklore separately, as though they were options, is to erase their common ground in a violence inflicted and a violence undergone, in a domination and a resignation always dependent upon each other."

ALBERT L. MICHAELS, "Revolutionary Cinema and the Self-Reflections on a Disappearing Class" *Journal of Latin American Lore*, Vol. 4, No. 1, 1978, pp. 129-134.

Couched in a discussion of the tension between the revolutionary nature of a film work and its mass accessibility, this essay moves on to a brief description of the Cuban film industry's attempts to overcome this tension. In the author's assessment, *Memories of Underdevelopment* is "not a call to arms" but rather a "depressing portrait" of a man and a city which have been supplanted by the new society. "Although its effect is not immediately revolutionary," the author concludes, it is "an excellent example of Marxist lore" (?) because of its "convincing picture" of the now virtually extinct Cuban middle class.

GERARDO CHIJONA, "Gutierrez Alea: An Interview," *Framework: A Film Journal*, No. 10, Spring, 1979, pp. 28-30, illus.

This excellent interview, translated from the Cuban film journal *Cine cubano*, sets *The Last Supper* in the context of other Cuban films about slavery and presents this director's commitment to works which "not only . . . help to interpret the world but also to transform it."

DAN GEORGAKAS, "Red Tape Blues," *Seven Days*, June 5, 1979, p. 34.

A review of *Death of a Bureaucrat* which draws on an interview with Tomas Gutierrez Alea during a 1978 film critics' tour to Cuba. Brief comments made on the self-satire found in Cuban newsreels not seen in the United States.

DENNIS WEST, "Slavery and Cinema in Cuba: The Case of Gutierrez Alea's *The Last Supper*," *The Western Journal of Black Studies*, Vol. 3, No. 2, Summer, 1979, pp. 128-133.

This intelligent and comprehensive review essay frames its discussion of *The Last Supper* with references to various tendencies in the scholarship relating to slavery and bondage.

ENRIQUE FERNANDEZ, " 'Witnesses Always Everywhere': The Rhetorical Strategies of *Memories of Underdevelopment*," *Wide Angle*, Vol. 4, No. 2, Winter, 1980.

A brief but extraordinary intelligent and fertile meditation on the issue of narrative point of view in Gutierrez Alea's most innovative and complex film, based on Nick Browne's rhetorical model for the structure of filmic narration. Fernandez outlines "the ways in which Sergio serves as narrative authority in both diegesis and discourse," proceeds to "discuss Sergio's move from narrator to protagonist as a moral repositioning of the spectator," and finally scrutinizes "the text's double function as historical witness and inscription."

CUBA—(Humberto Solas)

STEVEN KOVACS, "LUCIA: Style and Meaning in Revolutionary Film," *Monthly Review*, Vol. 27, No. 2, June, 1975, pp. 33-48.

This enthusiastic appreciation of Humberto Solas' three-part film dwells perhaps disproportionately on the first (and, thematically, the richest) episode: Lucia, 1895. Though he does make some important observations about the visual language of the film, Kovacs emphasizes meaning over style, attempting to elucidate the former in both national and international contexts. Despite a certain number of minor errors and misinterpretations, he largely succeeds.

ANNA MARIE TAYLOR, "LUCIA," *Film Quarterly*, Vol. XXVIII, No. 3, Winter-Spring, 1975, 53-59, illus.

A thoughtful and comprehensive appraisal of Solas' film which develops among other themes, that of "decolonization." Taylor is sensitive to the historical and cultural context of the film, to its thematic density and the variations in its film technique, and she takes pains to appraise the film's significance outside Cuba as well. She maintains that the film is not truly "feminist" because "it is neither told from a woman's psychological perspective . . . nor does it deeply explore women's oppression by patrtiarchal forms of society."

MARTA ALVEAR, "Every Point of Arrival is a Point of Departure: An Interview with Humberto Solas," *Jump/Cut* Special Section on Twney Years of Revolutionary Cuban Cinema, Part I, *Jump/Cut: A Review of Contemporary Cinema*, No. 19, December, 1978, pp. 27-31, 33, illus.

In this his most evtensive interview yet published in English, leading Cuban filmmaker Humberto Solas candidly discusses his personal history and the successes and failures of his filmmaking career from his early experimental work through *Cantata de Chile* (1975).

JOHN KING, "Humberto Solas: An Interview," *Framework: A Film Journal*, No. 10, Spring, 1979, pp. 24-27, illus. (Translated by Christine Weller.)

Centering mainly on the genesis and significance of *Cantata de Chile*, this interview also ranges over broader issues of cultural penetration and the difficulties of constituting an artistically and socially effective culture.

CUBA—(Pastor Vega)

Don Ranvaud, "Pastor Vega: An Interview," *Framework: A Film Journal*, No. 10, Spring, 1979, p. 23, illus.

In this brief interview, Vega, Head of International Relations for the Cuban Film Institute and a filmmaker himself, explains many basic aspects of film production and exhibition in Cuba clearly and succinctly.

Patricia Peyton and Carlos Broullon, "*Portrait of Teresa*: An Interview with Pastor Vega and Daisy Granados," *Cineaste*, Vol. X, No. 1, Winter, 1979-80, pp. 24-25, illus.

The director and lead actress of this polemical and popular Cuban film discusses its genesis and its reception within Cuba.

B. Ruby Rich, "*Portrait of Teresa*: Double Day, Double Standards," *Jump/Cut* Special Section, Twenty Years of Revolutionary Cuban Cinema, Part III, *Jump/Cut: A Review of Contemporary Cinema*, No. 22, May, 1980, pp. 30-32, illus.

This sensitive appraisal describes Teresa as "a woman poised in the moment of contradiction between revolutionary and traditional values, . . . vainly trying to satisfy both" and critiques the film's shift from questions of the double duties (home *and* workplace) to the morality of woman's sexual freedom, maintaining that the ending "falls into the trap of posing extremely private and individual solutions to what has been earlier established as a social problem." Finally, the author sets her assessment of *Portrait of Teresa* in the context of two other important Cuban features which deal with women's issues: *Lucia* (1968) and *One Way or Another* (1975).

JAMAICA—(General)

Julianne Burton, "The Harder They Come: Cultural Colonialism and the American Dream," *Jump/Cut*, Vol. I, No. 6, March-April, 1975, pp. 5-7.

An appraisal of this Jamaican feature (directed by Perry Henzell) which focuses on the political debate surrounding the film and offers a vindication of its often misunderstood visual style.

Claudia Dreifus, "Perry Henzell: The Perfect Ponder," *The Real Paper* (Boston), Vol. 4, No. 21, May, 1975, pp. 26-27, illus.

A revealing interview with the Jamaican-born, British-educated director of television commercials whose first feature film, *The Harder They Come*, caused an explosion at home and became a cult abroad.

Henzell discusses his filmmaking techniques (no shooting script, non-professional actors, improvised action, lightweight, hand-held camera), disavows any "Marxist intent" (seeing the film as simply anti-development, anti-consumer society) and discusses the two remaining films in his proposed Jamaican trilogy.

CANDACE SLATER, *"The Harder They Come* and the Picaresque Hero," *Review '76*, No. 18, Fall, 1976, pp. 88-91, illus.

This essay simultaneously inserts the film's protagonist into the picaresque tradition and differentiates him from it, concluding that Ivan is both more attractive and more tragic that the traditional picaresque hero, since "this latter-day *picaro* is condemned not because he defies society, but because he defies it alone."

MEXICO—(General)

MANUEL MICHEL, "Mexican Cinema: A Panoramic View," *Film Quarterly*, Vol. XVIII, No. 4, Summer, 1965, pp. 46-55, illus.

An excellent account of the prolific but ill-starred Mexican film industry from its origins through 1964 which focuses on outstanding films and filmmakers as well as on the organization and economics of the industry. Because the author is a filmmaker, film critic and film scholar in his native Mexico, his trenchant criticism of the corruption, unprincipled profiteering, and "fossilization" of the industry is a product of the heartfelt despair of the participant, rather than the patronizing or uncomprehending carpings of the outsider.

VIVIAN LASH, "Experimenting with Freedom in Mexico," *Film Quarterly*, Vol. XIX, No. 4, Summer, 1966, pp. 19-24, illus.

A necessary, if depressing, follow-up to Manuel Michel's article on the historical development of Mexican filmmaking and the contemporary situation, this article reports on the first (and second-to-last) feature-length Experimental Cinema Contest in Mexico City in July, 1965. In light of her descriptions and criticisms of the foremost films presented, and her summary of the state of *rigor mortis* paralyzing the official industry. Lash's unqualified optimism about the "success" of the contest is both incongruous and naive.

CARL J. MORA, "Mexico's Commercial Films: Sources for the Study of Social History," *Proceedings of the Pacific Coast Council on Latin American Studies*, Vol. 6, 1977-79, pp. 205-15.

A brief and rather routine survey which attempts, in the author's words, to present "a comprehensive overview of Mexican filmmaking while concurrently illustrating the extensive possibilities for study in this rich ... lode largely untapped by both Mexican and foreign scholars." Though neither goal is fully realized, the early historical section does contain some valuable information. Drastic changes in the industry after Lopez Portillo succeeded Luis Echeverria in the Mexican presidency (1976) are, unfortunately, outside the time frame of the essay.

JESUS SALVADOR TREVINO, "The New Mexican Cinema," *Film Quarterly*, Vol. XXXII, No. 3, Spring, 1979, pp. 26-37, illus.

A detailed and comprehensive assessment of the major films made under the "Echeverria experiment" (1970-1976) which sought to promote a socially-conscious, formallp imaginative, and economically viable national cinema under state auspices. This highly informative chronicle ends with reflections on changes facing film production in Mexico under the very different policies of Echeverria's successor, Lopez Portillo.

JESUS SALVADOR TREVINO, "Mexican Cinema: New Directors, New Films," *Somos*, May, 1979, pp. 32-37, illus.

In comparison with the longer *Film Quarterly* piece (see above), this is a slightly less detailed and more journalistic account of the "New Mexican Cinema" under President Luis Echeverria (1970-1976). Despite the threats it chronicles to this socially committed film movement, Trevino ends this version optimistically, finding potential solutions in international recognition, the inevitable oil boon, and collaborative efforts between Mexican, Chicano and Puerto Rican filmmakers.

YING YING WU, "Trying Times in Mexico," *Nuestro*, May, 1980, pp. 26-27, illus.

A brief summary of changes in the Mexican film industry under the regimes of Luis Echeverria (1971-1976) when the country's cinematic horizons expanded dramatically, and Lopez Portillo (1977-1982) when the industry was recognized in favor of the private sector, and production suffered a marked decline in both quantity and quality.

NICARAGUA—(General)

JULIANNE BURTON, "Filmmaking in Nicaragua: From Insurrection to INCINE: An Interview with Emilio Rodriguez Vazquez and Carlos Vicente Ibarra," *Cineaste*, Vol. 10, No. 2, Spring, 1980, pp. 28-31, illus.

A synthesis of interviews with two members of the Nicaraguan Film Institute (INCINE) conducted in New York and Havana in late

1979. Carlos Vicente Ibarra, a Nicaraguan and one of the leaders of the Film Institute, and Emilio Rodriguez Vazquez, a Puerto Rican volunteer who has remained in Nicaragua to work with INCINE, discuss filmmaking activity during the insurrectionary phase, the organization of INCINE, the first projects undertaken, and prospects for the future.

EVA COCKCROFT, "Film and Revolution: An Interview with Emilio Rodriguez," *Artworkers News*, Vol. 9, No. 7, March, 1980, pp. 28-29, illus.

A Puerto Rican filmmaker, working in Nicaragua in response to an appeal by the insurgent forces for volunteers trained in media, discusses filmmaking and cultural work in that country during the anti-Somoza insurrection and after the victory of the Sandinistas.

VENEZUELA—(General)

STEVE KOVACS, "Las Amazonas de Cine," *Sight and Sound*, Vol. 47, No. 2, Spring, 1978, pp. 91-93, illus.

A fascinating and unusual account of the three U.S.-educated women who run the Venezuelan National Film Office, focusing on their struggles and successes over the past decade in "developing a government policy for the creation and protection of a national film industry." The author attributes their "spectacular success, . . . possibly unrivaled in the history of cinema" to their nationalist, developmentalist mentality and insiders' approach and holds up their achievement as "an instructive example to those who wish to decolonize culture in the third world."

KENNETH BASCH, "Cinema Venezuela," *New Orleans Review*, Vol. 7, No. 2, Summer, 1980. pp. 185-189.

This essay sketches the background of state participation in the film industry and provides brief accounts of select films by Venezuela's leading filmmakers, beginning with Margot Benacerraf, whose feature-length documentary *Araya* won a prize at Cannes in 1958. Roman Challaud, Mauricio Wallerstein, Ivan Feo, Antonio Llerandi, Clemante de la Cerda, Michael Katz, and Carlos Rebolledo are among the current directors whose work is discussed. Particularly interesting is the account of Julio Neri's work in Super-8 and the role of this medium on the Venezuelan film scene. The dearth of material available in English on this increasingly important national film movement makes one wish that this article were longer and more detailed.

HISPANIC CINEMA IN U.S.A.

CHICANO—(General)

HARRY GAMBOA, JR., "Silver Screening the Barrio," *Equal Opportunity Forum*, November, 1978, pp. 6-7, illus.

A good basic introduction, written in a lively style, to the development of the Chicano presence in film and television as a response to "Mexploitation" in the Anglo-dominated media.

JASON C. JOHANSEN, "Third Annual Chicano Film Festival," *Nuestro*, October, 1978, pp. 40, 42, illus.

A candid, sensitive appraisal of the Third Annual Chicano Film Festival, held in San Antonio, Texas in August of 1978, as potentially a crucial moment of transition between periphery and mainstream.

LUIS TORRES, "*Raices de sangre*: First Feature Film Directed by a Chicano," *Somos*, *June/July*, 1978, pp. 16-19, illus.

An account of this first Chicano feature, made in Mexico by U.S.-born Jesus Trevino, which intersperses extensive quotations form the director.

SYLVIA MORALES, "Filming a Chicana Documentary," *Somos*, Vol. 2, No. 3, June, 1979, pp. 42-45, illus.

The genesis of the first documentary film made about and by Chicanas, *Bread and Roses*, a collaborative project by five Chicana women, as described by the director.

JULIO MORAN, "Films: Chicanos in New Era," *Somos*, Vol. 2, No. 2, March, 1979, pp. 12-15, illus.

An assessment of new possibilities for Chicano filmmakers and actors in Hollywood and independent productions.

JASON C. JOHANSEN, "Notes on Chicano Cinema," *Jump/Cut: A Review of Contemporary Cinema*, No. 23, October, 1980, pp. 9-10. (Reprinted from *Chicano Cinema Newsletter*, June, 1979.)

Based on the example of politically-committed filmmaking from Latin America, this brief essay, almost a manifesto, puts forth six priorities for Chicano film: demystification of the medium, decolonization of the viewers, self-reflexivity and open-endedness, "alternation of consciousness," serving as a catalyst for social change, and creating a Chicano film language.

SERGIO MUNOZ, editor, *Cine chicano: Primer acercamiento*, Cultural Supplement to *La Opinion*, No. 20, November 16, 1980, illus.

This impressive assessment of the accomplishments, limitations and future prospects of Chicano cinema contains articles by Jason Johansen, Jesus Trevino, Silvia Morales, Julio Moran, Jeff and Carlos Penichet, and Harry Gamboa, Jr., and concludes with a complete filmography. (Note: Spanish-language only.)

CHICANO—(Jesus Trevino)

JIM MILLER, "Chicano Cinema: Interview with Jesus Trevino," *Cineaste*, Vol. VIII, No. 3, Winter, 1977-78, pp. 38-41, illus.

This leading Chicano documentarist here discusses his background and the process of making his first feature-film, *Raices de sangre*, under the auspices of the state-run Mexican film industry.

CUBAN—(Exiles in U.S.)

SEBASTIAN DOMINGUEZ, " 'El Super,' Cuban Cinema in Exile Maturing: An Interview with Leon Ichaso and Orlando Jimenez-Leal," *Film Library Quarterly*, No. 12, No. 4, 1979, pp. 16-21, illus.

A disappontigly disconnected and at times contradictory interview, poorly edited and translated, with the makers of a subtle and powerful film about the Cuban exile community in New York.

DAN GEORGAKAS, *El Super*, *Cineaste*, Vol. 9, No. 4, 1979, pp. 49-51.

In addition to being a review of *El Super*, there are statements drawn from a radio interview with co-producer and co-director Leon Ichaso done by the author. The discussion takes in other films made by exiled Cubans and the attitude of Ichaso to films being made in Cuba.

PERIODICALS—SPANISH AND PORTUGUESE

CINE ALA DIA (Apartado 5.466, Sabana Grande. Caracas, Venezuela). Edited by a conscientious and politically committed editorial collective, *Cine al dia* has featured articles and interviews on New Latin American Cinema since 1968, while at the same time offering coverage of significant European and North American film activity. Especially valuable are the perceptive film reviews and the profuse, high quality stills.

CINE CUBANO (Calle 23, No. 1155, Habana, Cuba). Available in the United States through Smyrna Press, Box 1803-GPO Brooklyn, New York, NY 11202. Published continuously since 1960, this magazine is the oldest and one of the best of the Latin American film journals. An excellent source of information on filmmaking in Cuba and other Latin American countries, this journal also deals with worldwide film history and activity from a consistently Marxist perspective.

CINE OJO (Ulises Estrella, Seccion de Cine, Casa de Cultura Ecuatoriana, Quito, Ecuador). A new journal by the editor of the now discontinued 1 X 1: *CINE Y MEDIOS DE COMUNICACION*.

FILME CULTURA (Rua Mayrink Veiga 29, 2° andar, Rio de Janeiro, RJ, Brazil). This leading Brazilian film journal focuses on national cinema, and counts among the members of its editorial board such well-known critics as David Neves, Ismail Xavier, Jean-Claude Bernardet and Jose Carlos Avellar.

FORMATO 16 (Apartado 60-1775, Estafeta El Dorado, Panama, Republic of Panama). Published by the Educational Film Group of the national university since 1976, this journal carries articles and interviews on film activity in Panama as well as in other sections of Latin America.

HABLEMOS DE CINE (Libertadores 199-27, Lima, Peru). Founded in the mid-sixties, this magazine has moved from a "cosmopolitan" and "auteurist" critical perspective to greater commitment to the New Latin American Cinema and, as a result of the politicization of the film movement in Peru, to an increasingly Marxist perspective. Particularly high quality interviews.

IMAGENES (Corregio 12, Mexico 19, D.F., Mexico). Directed by leading critic and historian Emilio Garcia Riera, this journal features articles on European and Hollywood cinema as well as filmmaking activity in Latin America.

OCTUBRE (Taller de Cine Octubre, Trinidad Langarica, Apartado Postal 19-495, Mexico 19, D.F., Mexico). Despite its sporadic publication schedule, this is a very valuable journal which publishes extensive articles and interviews with such leading figures of the Latin American film movement as Julio Garcia Espinosa (Cuba), Miguel Littin (Chile), Ruy Guerra (Brazil), Carlos Alvarez (Colombia), Gerardo Vallejo (Argentina/Panama), Jorge Sanjines (Bolivia), as well as articles on Mexican cinema and political cinema throughout the world.

SEGUNDO TRANCO (Apartado Aerea 11883, Bogota, Colombia). Filmmaker, historian and theorist Carlos Alvarez initiated this publication—more of a newsletter than a journal, more polemical than informational—in late 1980 as the successor to two other now-defunct Colombia film magazines.

The following Latin American film journals have ceased publication: 1 X 1: *CINE Y MEDIOS DE COMMUNICACION* (Ecuador), *OJO AL CINE* (Colombia), *CINEMATOGRAFO* (Peru), *FILM/HISTORIA* (Bolivia).

The following English language journals are cited in this bibliography or cover Latin American films with some regularity:

Afterimage, American Behavioral Scientist, American Film Institute Education Newsletter, American Film, Americas, Artworkers News, Atlas, The Black Scholar, Chamba Notes, Chicano Cinema Caucus Newsletter, Cine-Tracts, Cineaste, Cinema, Cinema Papers, CTVE (Cinema-TV-Digest), Diacritics, The Drama Review, Evergreen (defunct), *Film and History, Film Comment, Film Library Quarterly, Film Quarterly, Film Society Review* (defunct), *Film Studies Annual, Filmmakers' Newsletter, Films and Filming, Framework, Harper's, Ideologies and Literature, Index On Censorship, International Film Guide, Issues, Jeune/Young Cinema and Theatre, Journal of Latin American Lore, Journal of Modern Literature, Jump/Cut, Latin American Literary Review, Latin American Perspectives, Luso-Brazilian Review, Millenium Film Journal, Monograph, Monthly Review, Movietone News, New Boston Review, New Orleans Review, New Statesman, Nuestro, Proceedings of the Pacific Coast Council on Latin American Studies, Quarterly Review of Film Studies, The Real Paper* (defunct), *Review,*

Screen, Seven Days (defunct), *Sight and Sound, Socialist Review, Somos, Take One, The Texas Quarterly, Towards Revolutionary Art* (defunct), *The Western Journal of Black Studies.*

For current addresses of these periodicals, the best guides are the directories published by R. R. Bowker, the annual *International Film Guide,* and the annual *The International Directory of Little Magazines and Small Presses.* Individuals who need further assistance in finding an address for a magazine or distributor should send a self-addressed stamped envelope and one dollar to *Cineaste,* 200 Park Avenue South, New York, NY 10003, U.S.A.

For current addresses of distributors of Latin American films contact Cine Information, 215 West 90th Street (9c), New York, NY 10024 or Media Network, 208 West 13th Street, New York, NY 10011.

FILMMAKERS INDIVIDUALLY CITED

Argentina:	Eduardo de Gregorio, Raymundo Gleyzer, Jorge Preloran, Fernando Solanas, and Octavio Getino.
Bolivia:	Antonio Eguino and Jorge Sanjines.
Brazil:	Bruno Barreto, Luiz Carlos Barreto, Alberto Cavalcanti, Joaquim Pedro de Andrade, Carlos Diegues, Ruy Guerra, Humberto Mauro, Nelson Pereira dos Santos, Glauber Rocha, and Orlando Senna.
Chile:	Patricio Guzman, Miguel Littin, Ral Ruiz, and Antonio Skarmeta.
Cuba:	Santiago Alvarez, Julia Garcia Espinosa, Sergio Giral, Manuel Octavio Gomez, Sara Fomez, Tomas Gutierrez Alea, Humberto Solas, and Pastor Vega.
Jamaica:	Perry Henzell.
USA (Chicano):	Jesus Trevino.